start
with
what
if

Published in the United States by Five Leaf Clover Publishing, LLC
174 Adams Street, Unit 3, Newton, MA 02458
FiveLeafCloverPublishing.com

First Five Leaf Clover Publishing Press Edition, 2025
First Printing

ISBN 979-8-9887762-2-2 (paperback)
ISBN 979-8-9887762-3-9 (ebook)

Weekly Questions to Spark
Immediate Change and Growth

start
with

what
if

Pause. Question. Go.

DOUG FLEENER

To my family—Joanna, Kate, Jane, and Lyla.

I love watching you grow and evolve. You make me deeply proud. Thank you for being the living answer to my best What If questions. Because of you, I keep asking, keep growing, and keep loving more deeply than I ever imagined.

To the many people in my life who became teachers, even when I didn't recognize them as such. Your lessons, challenges, and examples shaped me in ways I carry forward every day.

And to the readers of this book—thank you for opening yourself to new questions and possibilities. May the What Ifs you ask lead to better days and a life you love living.

CONTENTS

A Change & Growth Inflection Chapter:
Your Thinking Follows the Doing   99

A Change & Growth Inflection Chapter: It's Not a Straight Line   117

A Change & Growth Inflection Chapter: What if this
week, you didn't respond when you felt compelled to?   145

A Change & Growth Inflection Chapter:
Practice Relentless Simplicity   163

INTRODUCTION

This book is built for momentum, for change, for growth—
and likely, for you.

Let's be honest. Most books like this overpromise.

They claim they'll change your life. Make you rich. Maybe
even better looking. (Those always got me.)

And maybe they could. But life doesn't change in theory. It
changes in real time. In one moment, one decision, and, most
importantly, one action at a time.

That's why this book won't hand you a checklist or give
you the answers. What it will provide you with is something
better: the right questions.

Each week, you'll get one "What If" designed to spark
reflection, create clarity, and move you forward.

If you want to change, grow, act, or simply ask better questions
about the life you're building, you're in the right place.

If you're looking for a better way forward—at work, in relationships, or just in daily life—this book was written for you.

Why Me?

Years ago, my life was a mess. I was drinking and using drugs
every day. I was utterly lost.

It was the Monday after the New York Giants had defeated
the Denver Broncos in Super Bowl XXI. Midday, I was just
waking up—head pounding—when I heard a voice over a
loudspeaker: "We'll be landing at Dallas–Fort Worth airport."

I opened my eyes and realized I was in the center seat of a plane. I reached into my pocket and pulled out a thick wad of cash. How did it get there? More importantly, how did I get there?

Then it hit me. Another blackout. Another low. I was a twenty-eight-year-old drug addict, alcoholic, and thief. The money was what remained from a family marine supply business I'd bankrupted with a daily cocaine habit.

It was the worst day of my life. But it would turn out to be the most important.

When I got home, I had to face my father—my business partner—who had discovered I'd been stealing from the company. He knew I drank but not how bad my drug problem had become.

I ended up in a recovery meeting, where someone asked me a simple question that would change everything:

"What if you just lived today without a drink or a drug?"

That question didn't solve my problems. But it cracked the door open. It gave me something small and possible to hold onto. A single change in thinking that turned into action and, eventually, a life I never thought I'd get to live.

That was my first What If moment. I've been asking and sharing better questions ever since. I knew I needed to share this incredibly simple approach with others.

Real change doesn't come from knowing more; it comes from doing something different.

How This Book Is Different

This is not a typical book. (More on that in chapter 4.)

The first four chapters will give you the foundation: what What If moments are, the simple rule that makes them work, why small actions create big changes, and how to use this book effectively. Then we'll jump into fifty-two weeks of questions designed to move you forward.

This book is built on one simple belief: Big changes start with small, intentional questions. Not resolutions. Not ten-year plans. Just one new thought each week that shifts how you see things and nudges you into action.

Questions like:

What if this week, you lived without comparing yourself to others?

What if this week, you celebrated someone or something just because?

What if this week, you didn't let someone's bad mood or negativity affect you?

What if this week, you saw how you always have more choices than you first thought?

Some of these will challenge you. Some will surprise you. Some might not apply. A few might even annoy you. (Those are usually the ones worth sitting with.)

But if you're like the people I spend time with, you'll start to notice something. These questions don't just inspire you. They move you. They help you to see what you've been avoiding, they open new paths, and they prompt you to take more intentional action.

That's the power of What If.

And that's what this book is here to offer—one week, one question, one step at a time.

You're one question away.

What if we start now?

THE POWER OF WHAT IF MOMENTS

There was a moment when I almost walked away from everything—my coaching, my speaking, the work I felt called to do.

I'd been at it for about a year after leaving my job at Bose Corporation. Saying it wasn't going well would be generous. I was burning through our savings. Confidence was slipping. I wasn't sure if I should keep going or whether I could.

Then I got a call from a headhunter. He thought I'd be perfect for a leadership role at Circuit City. (If you don't know what that was, stay with me. It's part of the story.) I figured this might be the answer to the question I'd been asking: Am I supposed to keep doing this, or is it time to go back to what I know?

I updated my résumé, dug out my suit from the back of the closet, and went to the interview.

It was a disaster.

The interviewer was distracted and disinterested. It felt like he was forced to meet with me. Near the end, he told me I'd have to take a "step back" from where I'd been at Bose. It wasn't a step back. It was a joke.

It's the closest I've ever come to saying something bad in an interview, except my mother wouldn't have approved. But I smiled, told him I'd think about it, and thanked him for his time.

As I walked down the hallway from his office, it hit me:

What if I did whatever it takes to make my business succeed?

I had tried a lot. But I hadn't gone all in.

That one question changed my perspective. It opened up my energy, my options, and my mindset. I reached into my briefcase, pulled out the stack of résumés I'd printed, and dropped them in the trash can by the elevator. Which felt great.

That was my What If moment. I never looked back.

It didn't solve everything. It wasn't an instant breakthrough. But something shifted. I walked out of that building fully committed. All in.

That moment didn't just change my decision. It changed how I worked and lived. I've spent the last three decades helping people and companies use questions like that to move forward with more clarity, confidence, and purpose. (Ironically, Circuit City itself didn't move forward—they eventually went bankrupt.)

When Questions Become Possibilities

Most of us think life changes through big, dramatic events. But most changes start small. It begins when you pause mid-thought, mid-struggle, mid-routine—and ask a different kind of question.

Not a regret. Not a complaint. Not an excuse. A possibility.

What if I tried this instead?
What if I didn't quit today?
What if there's a better way?

That's a What If moment. A mental pivot that reframes the way you see yourself, your options, and what's possible next.

These moments don't scream. They whisper. And most people miss them. But if you catch them, they can change everything.

Your Brain on What If

You don't have to force these moments. They already show up. When you're on your way home from work and find yourself unhappy or frustrated. During a quiet conversation, when something inside you stirs. When you can't stop thinking about that one thing you've been avoiding or want to do.

The problem isn't that these moments are rare. The problem is that we miss or dismiss them. We tell ourselves it's too late. Or too early. Or too much.

But you don't need certainty. You need movement. And a What If moment gives you just enough clarity and hope to take the next step.

Science backs this up. In psychology, this type of questioning is called cognitive reappraisal. It's pausing to reinterpret a situation in a way that gives you more agency and possibility.

Studies published in the *Journal of Experimental Psychology* demonstrate that hypothetical questions like "What if . . . ?" can significantly enhance problem-solving, decision-making, and emotional regulation. They don't just change how you think. They change how you act.

Because once your brain sees a new possibility, your behavior starts to follow.

The Looking-Back Trap

Everyone asks What If questions. But most people use them to look backward:

What if I had taken that job?
What if I hadn't said that?
What if I had started sooner?

Those questions trap you in regret.
The kind that matters most look forward:

What if I ran with that idea I've been thinking about?
What if I stopped carrying guilt I no longer need?
What if I lived this week like I already believe it is possible?

These are possibility questions. They don't fix the past. They change your perspective. And when you take action, they transform your future.

Someone I once worked with was on the edge of burnout. Long hours. Endless issues. No clear win in sight. She was debating whether to leave the company and felt like she had nothing left to give.

We were talking about it one day, when she paused and said, "What if I just need to change how I am working?" That one question reframed it well.

She didn't resign. She restructured. Delegated differently. Reset her expectations. Changed how she traveled and led her team.

Three months later, same job. Different energy.

One moment. One shift. That's the power of asking the right "what if."

What If moments are already in your life. They're happening in quiet thoughts, tiny nudges, half-formed hopes. This book will help you learn how to change and grow because of them.

So here's your first What If question:

What if the small question you ask today changes your tomorrow?

Let's find out.

THE WHAT IF RULE

The What If Rule is the foundation of this book. It's based on one simple principle: You can always create better perspectives and options.

No matter what's happening in your work or life, you can pause and ask a question that helps you view your situation through a new lens. It's not a trick. It's a skill. And once you begin using it, you realize you're capable of creating more clarity, more ideas, and better outcomes in almost any situation.

You won't always find the perfect answer. But you will always be able to create something that moves you forward. Something better than a default reaction. Something more useful, more grounded.

Many people believe their mindset is set in stone. That they either have clarity or they don't. That they're calm or reactive. That the day is either ruined or it isn't.

But that's not how it works. Change doesn't come from waiting for better circumstances. Change begins when you ask a better question.

How the What If Rule Works

The What If Rule has three simple components:

The Rule – You can always create better perspectives and options.

The Method – Ask What If questions as interrupters.

The Framework – Pause. Question. Go.

When you feel stuck, reactive, frustrated, or overwhelmed or are facing a challenge or even an opportunity, use What If questions as interrupters—breaking the automatic pattern before it takes over. Pause the default response, ask a What If question that opens up new possibilities, and then act based on your new perspective.

When Life Hits You Early

Let's say you wake up already behind. Three stressful messages on your phone. No clean clothes. The kitchen's a mess. And the day hasn't even started yet.

The instinct is to tense up, grumble, or shut down. You mentally rewrite the whole day as hard, rushed, and frustrating, and assume it's going to keep getting worse.

That's the automatic reaction. It's natural.

But applying the What If Rule means using a What If question as an interrupter. You pause the automatic reaction and ask yourself a different question.

What if I didn't let the first ten minutes decide the whole day?

What if I tackled just one thing at a time, and let the momentum build?

What if I gave myself the same grace I'd give someone else?

It doesn't erase the mess. But it changes how you show up in it. And that shift changes what happens next.

Flipping the What If Switch

Most people ask What If questions all the time. But they usually go negative.

What if I mess this up?
What if nothing ever changes?
What if I'm not good enough?

That kind of questioning leads to a racing mind, self-doubt, and more frustration. But when you use What If intentionally as an interrupter, it becomes a tool. It gives you a way to reframe your perspective, to reinterpret what's happening, and to choose how you move forward.

Psychologists refer to this ability to shift perspectives as cognitive flexibility. It's one of the most essential traits in resilience, problem solving, and growth. Researchers such as Carol Dweck and Ellen Langer have demonstrated that individuals who intentionally reframe their thinking experience greater feelings of capability and reduced feelings of being stuck. They perform better under pressure. They recover more quickly after setbacks.

And neuroscience supports this. When you ask a question like "What if there's another way to see this?" your brain's default mode network activates. This is the part of your brain responsible for imagining different futures and alternate outcomes. Your brain is wired to explore possibilities. It just needs a spark.

What If questions are that spark.

What If at Home

A friend of mine told me about a rough morning she had with her teenage daughter. Tension was high. Voices were raised. The argument ended with slammed doors and a lingering sense of frustration.

Later that day, she paused and asked herself, *What if my daughter isn't just being difficult? What if she's scared about something and doesn't know how to talk about it?*

She used the What If question as an interrupter—pausing her frustration to create space for a different approach. That one question changed her perspective. Instead of confronting her daughter out of frustration, she approached with curiosity. Her daughter eventually opened up. It turned out the fight wasn't about the surface issue at all. Something had been happening at school, and it was bothering her.

The question didn't erase the conflict, but it created a new path through it. Same people. Same event. Entirely different outcome.

The Rule Versus the Moment

Every What If moment is an opportunity to apply the rule. But here's the key:

The What If Rule is the mindset. It's the belief that you can always create better perspectives and options, no matter what's happening.

A What If moment is when you use it. Sometimes those moments catch you off guard. You're mid-frustration or mid-decision, and something inside you pauses. A question shows up. You shift.

Other times, you create the moment on purpose. You use the rule to chart a different way forward.

This book is about both: the mindset and the application, the rule and the moments.

It's Relentlessly Simple

You don't need a complicated system. You don't need perfect conditions. You just need to remember: You can apply the What If Rule anywhere and at any time. At home, when you're in a tense conversation with your partner. At work, when you're trying to figure out a better process or improve a presentation. In your head, when you're upset or want to do something better.

You can use the rule in just a few seconds. You can use it without anyone knowing. You can use it whether things are going well or not.

That's what makes this different from most personal development approaches. You're not building toward something. You're using it right now.

You already have the questions. This book will help you choose better ones. You already have the moments. This book will help you act on them.

This book is a weekly invitation to practice the What If Rule in fifty-two different life situations. Now, let's talk about how to put it into action.

YOU'RE ONE ACTION AWAY

Kayla O'Reilly used TikTok like millions of other users—posting dancing videos and voice-overs. Then one day she had a What If moment: What if I started doing something every day after work so I wasn't just living for the weekend?

It was a thought that's crossed millions of minds. But Kayla did something more. She took action. She posted on TikTok that it was Day One of her doing something every day after work so she wouldn't just live for the weekend. The next day, she posted Day Two. And she kept going.

She went viral. As of this writing, her Day Eleven post has had more than 5 million views.

She didn't start posting to go viral. She started because she wanted to feel different, to shift something inside her. And she knew the secret most people miss: You don't think your way into a new way of acting. You act your way into a new way of thinking.

That's what this chapter is about.

The Gap Between Ideas and Impact

The What If Rule is powerful because it opens up better perspectives and options. But none of that matters if you don't take action.

Most people wait to feel ready before they start. They wait until they're more confident, more organized, more inspired.

But real change never works like that.

Confidence doesn't show up before you act. It shows up because you did.

That's why the shift doesn't end with a question. It starts there. But what happens next is what creates the transformation. The moment you take even the smallest action, your brain gets a new signal: *Something is different. We're moving. We're not just sitting here.*

And that action doesn't need to be big.

It can be sending the email you've been avoiding. Going for a walk when you don't feel like it. Choosing not to reply to a comment that will only lead to frustration. Or, like Kayla, doing something small after work instead of slipping into autopilot.

Every time you take an action that aligns with a better perspective, you reinforce that mindset. You make it easier to choose again tomorrow.

That's how transformation happens: one shift, then one choice, then one step.

Why Action Changes Everything

You can always create better perspectives and options. That's the power of the What If Rule. But what turns that possibility into something real is what you do next.

Think of each What If question as a doorway. Asking the question opens it. Walking through it is what makes the difference.

What Kayla tapped into—without realizing it—is something psychologists have long known. When you take consistent, values-aligned action, your beliefs start to follow. It's called behavioral activation. And it's been shown to reduce anxiety, increase motivation, and even shift long-term habits.

But here's the thing: The activation must happen.

No matter how good the question is, no matter how much clarity it gives you, it's the action that cements the shift. Most people get stuck here. They want the change, but they overthink the first move. They tell themselves it needs to be perfect or profound.

It doesn't. You just need to start.

You Don't Need the Whole Map

The brain loves certainty. It wants to know how things will play out before it's willing to begin. However, growth doesn't work that way. Clarity is often a result, not a prerequisite.

The goal isn't to predict everything. It's to build trust with yourself by taking action.

You don't need a five-year vision. You need a next step.

That's what each chapter of this book will offer you. Not just a question to think about but a moment to act on. Not a massive, life-changing effort. Just a meaningful shift you can make.

And here's the best part: Once you start moving, your brain catches up. You feel different because you're doing something different. And the more you act, the easier it becomes to keep acting.

You begin to realize something most people never do: You don't have to wait to become the person you want to be. You can start acting like that person right now.

Change and Growth Always Start with Today

You're one action away. Starting today.

That's one of my favorite sayings. Growth starts with action. Change begins with action. Every good thing starts with action. And all of it only happens when you act today.

I never assume someone is broken. I just assume that most people want to grow, to be happier, and to feel more alive.

This book explores what's possible. These weekly questions aren't here to point out what you lack. They're here to help you reconnect to your potential—one What If question, and one meaningful action, at a time.

So when a question speaks to you, act on it. Let it move you, even just a little. That's how the momentum begins.

Because no matter where you are or what you're facing:

You're one action away.

Starting today.

And your next action is to discover the different ways to use this book.

HOW TO USE THIS BOOK
AND WHY IT WORKS

There's no single right way to read this book.

Some people will jump straight to the week they need most. Others will start at the beginning and move one week at a time. Some will read the whole thing first, then circle back and take it week by week.

All of that works.

What matters is not how you read the book. What matters is what you do with it.

This book is about creating weekly What If moments—those pivotal instances when you pause and ask a different question and something shifts. These weekly questions aren't designed to fix what's broken or point out what you're missing. They're here to help you intentionally create better perspectives and options, one meaningful question at a time.

And they serve a dual purpose. Each weekly What If chapter not only helps you grow and take action but also gives you a real-life chance to practice the What If Rule: Pause. Question. Go.

This isn't just a mindset shift. It's a rhythm. A weekly opportunity to slow down, shift your thinking, and take a clear next step. Over time, this becomes a skill you can use anywhere, anytime—not just once a week.

Some of the questions will hit perfectly. Some won't apply to you. The key is to stay open to what is and what could be.

The Weekly Rhythm

Each weekly chapter follows a simple flow. It begins with a What If question, followed by stories and insights that help you see the situation from a different perspective. Then there are two paths forward: One offers clear action steps you can take right now, and the other gives you space to reflect and notice patterns before you're ready to act. There's also a final spot for committing to an action for the week.

Choose your path. Take what serves you, and leave what doesn't. The goal is simple: Make one meaningful change per week that compounds into a better life.

Your Weekly Approach

Pick a consistent day and time to read. Sunday night. Monday morning. Friday before the weekend. There's no perfect answer. Just choose something that works for you.

Read the weekly question and decide how you want to engage with it. You might dive in immediately and take action that day. Or you might let it sit with you, riding along through the week, quietly shaping how you approach conversations, decisions, and how you show up for yourself. The question will do its job either way.

Take one meaningful step. You don't need to overhaul your life. Just find one small action or insight you can carry into the week. Write it down. Say it out loud. Share it with someone. Or just live it.

Come back to it when needed. You'll experience the

questions differently over time. A chapter that barely registered in January might hit much harder in August. That's not failure. That's growth.

You'll miss a week. Or two. That's not a problem. Life gets busy. Don't worry about it. Don't try to catch up. Just pick up where you left off. Or open to whatever question speaks to you right now. You don't have to follow the order. You just have to keep showing up.

What About Journaling?

Journaling is optional. But powerful.

Write the question at the top of a blank page. Give yourself ten minutes. Don't worry about spelling or structure. Just write.

Or use a journaling app like Day One. Create a journal called "What If." Then, once a week, create an entry with the question and your thoughts. If you journal daily, you can use the question as a theme and build on it throughout the week.

Other people like to discuss the question with a partner or a team. Some bring it into coaching sessions or meetings.

There's no single right way. The only wrong way is to do nothing with it.

Your What If Journey Starts Now

This book contains fifty-two weekly questions and twelve foundational chapters on creating and living with "What If" Moments, plus eight chapters that show how to apply the "What If" Rule in specific roles and situations.

You don't need to follow a perfect sequence or memorize

anything. You'll feel the shift as you move through the questions.

What if we begin?

1.

WHAT IF THIS WEEK, YOU DID ONE THING THAT YOU'VE BEEN PUTTING OFF?

I've always felt that the thought of doing laundry is worse than actually doing it. Every time I walk past the pile, I swear it yells at me! It reminds me of what I haven't done. And it only gets bigger.

The same thing used to happen with expense reports. I'd let them sit until it wasn't just time-consuming—it was costing me real money. The pile grew, and so did the pressure.

It's easy to spot this pattern everywhere. A difficult conversation that goes unspoken for weeks. A project that stays untouched because we're unsure we'll do it well. Going through the stack of mail that's starting to tower over you.

Sometimes the thing we're avoiding only takes ten minutes to complete. But the longer we delay, the more it drains us. It takes up space in our minds, affects our mood, and makes us feel like we're falling behind, even when everything else is getting done.

I've stopped calling it procrastination. That word comes loaded with judgment. I've coached too many people who say things like "I'm just a procrastinator," as if it's a fixed part of who they are. It's not. It's just something they've been avoiding. And avoidance can be addressed.

The Pile That Yells Back

Avoidance isn't just about the thing you're not doing. It's about the energy it quietly consumes. When something keeps getting pushed to next week's list, it weighs more every time. It grows in your mind and shapes your self-talk.

That expense report sitting on my desk wasn't just paperwork—it was a daily reminder that I was behind, disorganized, maybe even irresponsible. Every time I saw it, I felt a little worse about myself. That's the hidden cost of putting things off. It's not just the task itself. It's what carrying it around does to your confidence.

But when you finally do it—even just a small step—you feel different. You stop the draining feeling. You get relief and maybe even momentum.

The Anti-Avoidance Fix

Most people who avoid something imagine that starting will take willpower or discipline. But what helps is removing the mental weight of delay. Avoidance isn't about laziness. It's about emotion. The task might feel unclear, unpleasant, or like it says something about who you are. When you name that, the grip loosens.

What helps most is shrinking the decision. Instead of committing to the whole task, commit to ten minutes. Or just one small part. That shift turns avoidance into progress.

I finally solved my expense report problem by creating a

simple rule: I couldn't start my weekend until that week's report was done. That small change worked. I never got behind again. Not because I became more disciplined but because I made the task easier to do than to avoid.

You don't need to become someone who finishes everything right away. You just need to take back your power to face one thing that's been lingering. That single action can completely change how you feel about yourself.

The Fast Path to Getting It Done

1. Identify the one thing you've been putting off.
Pick something manageable. Not your entire backlog. Just one task that's been sitting there too long.

2. Understand why you've avoided it.
Ask yourself why this one task keeps getting pushed. Is it annoying? Unclear? Intimidating? Naming the reason helps reduce its grip.

3. Schedule it and shrink it.
Pick a day and time. If it feels overwhelming, commit to just ten minutes or one small part of it. Make starting easier than avoiding.

4. Notice how It feels to be done.
Pay attention to the relief, the momentum, or the confidence that comes from finally handling it. That feeling is your reward for facing what you've been avoiding.

The Awareness Path to Breaking the Delay

Notice what you've been putting off this week. Pay attention to how it affects your energy and mindset when you think about it. Sometimes, the mental energy spent avoiding something is greater than the energy needed to just do it. What would it feel like to just get it off your list?

Your What If Action

This week I will _____

_____

_____

_____

_____

_____

_____

_____

_____

2.

WHAT IF THIS WEEK, YOU ADDED A LITTLE SPONTANEOUS FUN JUST BECAUSE YOU CAN?

I was having lunch with some employees of a company I was working with when one of the attendees said something that stopped me. She talked about her "superpower" being spontaneous fun. That was a new one for me.

She explained that when she feels under pressure or when too much is going on in her life, she "throws on her cape" and does something fun. Her favorite example? The time she stopped by herself at a miniature golf course on the way home from a stressful day at work.

I loved it. Not just the image of someone playing mini golf alone, but the idea of treating fun like a superpower you can activate when you need it most.

Most people do the opposite. When life gets intense, fun is the first thing to go. They save it for weekends or vacations, when they have permission or perfect timing. But she had figured out something different: Spontaneous fun isn't a luxury—it's a tool. It doesn't wait for the right moment—it creates one.

The only question is whether you'll throw on your cape when you need it.

The Permission Problem

Most people associate fun with events, free time, or a time of permission. They believe they need to earn it—or that fun only counts if it's planned. But spontaneous fun is different. It's a reset, not a reward—a spark, not a schedule. You don't need more time. You just need to stop skipping the moments that are already there.

Often, those moments show up after the workday ends. That window where you could try something different instead of sliding into your usual routine. You could take a walk with music instead of turning on the TV. Say yes to the impromptu invite. Play a game. Try a new place. Do something you wouldn't normally do on a weeknight—not because it's productive but because it breaks the pattern.

That's what makes it fun. It's unexpected. Unnecessary. And somehow, precisely what you needed.

Fun in the Margins

Most people don't avoid fun. They just don't make space for it. After a long day, it's easy to default to the couch, scroll your phone, or power through your to-do list. But that window between work and bedtime, or when your evening is open, or even before work or school, is the perfect place for spontaneous fun.

Treat yourself to something different. Play miniature golf on a random Tuesday. Or a spontaneous game of tennis or nine holes of golf with a friend. Check out a local band or a pop-up event, or spend an evening at the museum. Skip making dinner and turn it into a picnic. Invite your partner, a friend, your kids, or just go solo. You don't have to wait for a weekend or a vacation to enjoy something playful.

Fun doesn't always show up as a plan. Sometimes it shows up as a small spark, an idea you'd normally skip. This week, don't brush past the thought. Say yes before your brain has a chance to overrule it.

The Fast Path to Spontaneous Joy

1. Catch yourself when you're about to say no to a fun idea or thought.
That quick "not now" reflex? Notice it.

2. Say yes to a playful impulse. Even a small one.
Follow the impulse. Play the game, take the detour, try the new thing. Go play miniature golf while wearing a cape. Choose the option that sounds fun over the one that sounds sensible.

3. Invite someone else into the moment.
Fun spreads. It breaks the tension. It's one of the fastest ways to reconnect.

4. Notice how it changes your energy.
Let the moment of fun carry forward into the rest of your day or week. Let it be part of the rhythm, not a break from it.

The Awareness Path to Fun Opportunities
Catch yourself in your routine this week. The moment you

automatically start winding down, reach for the remote, or fall into your usual evening pattern, pause. Is there something fun you could do instead? Could you invite a friend, a partner, or your kids to join you in doing something small and different? You do not need a big plan. You just need to be willing to shift the default. That is where fun often begins.

Your What If Action

This week I will

3

WHAT IF THIS WEEK, YOU SAW HOW YOU ALWAYS HAVE MORE CHOICES THAN YOU FIRST THOUGHT?

One of the benefits of working with a coach or mentor is how they help you see options you didn't even know were there.

You talk about a challenge or problem. Maybe you're in a stuck place, a "this feels like the only way" kind of moment. And within minutes, they're pointing out three other directions you hadn't considered.

They don't magically create those choices. They just help you see them.

That breaks you out of the first idea that grabbed your mind. It slows you down just long enough to scan the whole picture. It helps you see that your current thinking isn't wrong. It's just incomplete.

You can learn to do that for yourself.

When Your Field of Vision Shrinks

Most people aren't out of options. They're just not seeing them. It's easy to react to what's familiar or assumed without pausing to consider what else might be possible. When your view narrows, so do your choices.

That's what this week is about—expanding your perception before you commit to action.

Start with something simple. You open the fridge. Nothing looks good. You tell yourself, "I guess I'll just have cereal again." That's the default. The fast path. But not necessarily the best one.

You could cook. Order. Ask someone. Skip the meal. Prep for tomorrow instead. You don't need to do them all. You just need to name more than one option.

Choice lives in awareness, not just availability.

When Life Opens Up

I had an employee whose direct report was consistently under-performing. His instinct was to move the person out and bring in someone stronger. That was his only perceived option.

We listed out some others. He could coach the person for another quarter. Try a different communication style. Pair them with a peer mentor. Shift responsibilities slightly to fit their strengths. Have a conversation with human resources about a formal development plan.

He didn't have to do all of them. But suddenly, it wasn't just "keep or replace." He saw multiple ways forward. That shift in thinking made him a better leader—not just in that moment but in every future decision.

The same goes for personal life.

A woman once told me she'd always had a rough relationship with her brother. Their mother was the glue that held them together. After their mother passed, the woman figured that was it. With no reason to stay in touch, she assumed she and her brother would simply drift apart or stay distant for good.

But then she found herself thinking about their mom. A memory came back. Then another. And instead of keeping them to herself, she started texting them to her brother. Just short, simple messages: "Remember how she used to make cinnamon toast on Saturday mornings?" "I found that old birthday card she wrote you."

There was no big moment. Just a slow shift. The connection they shared through their mom began to grow into something new between the two of them, all because instead of defaulting to disconnection, the woman looked for another way it could go. And it changed everything.

Sometimes, just seeing another choice is enough to bring back momentum.

This week, that's your challenge. In any moment where you feel stuck, cornered, frustrated, or bored, pause and ask what other ways this could go.

You don't need to act on all the ideas or even pick a new one. Just notice that you had more options than you thought.

That's where freedom is.

The Fast Path to Expanding Your Options

1. Catch your first reaction.
When you hear yourself say "I have to" or "I can't," stop. That's usually the first sign you're narrowing your options.

2. Ask what other ways this could go.
Train your brain to move beyond the default. Don't ask whether there's another option. Ask what the options are.

List at least two.

3. Pick your next move intentionally.
Once you've expanded your field of view, choose the option that best fits the moment, not just the one that arrived first.

4. Reflect on how the shift felt.
Was the original plan still right? Great. But was there something better once you looked around? How did that feel?

The Awareness Path to Seeing Beyond Your First Choice
This week, notice when you slip into autopilot decision-making. Watch your language. "I can't," "I have to," and "There's no other way" are often lies your brain tells for convenience. When you hear them, pause and ask what other ways this could go. The moment you do that, your world widens.

Your What If Action

This week I will _____

_____

_____

_____

_____

4.

WHAT IF THIS WEEK, YOU STARTED OR CHANGED A ROUTINE THAT YOUR FUTURE SELF WILL THANK YOU FOR?

Your routines shape your life. Even the ones you never meant to create.

Most people don't consciously build their daily rhythm. They fall into it. A few repeated choices turn into a pattern. The pattern becomes familiar. And without realizing it, that routine starts calling the shots.

But routines aren't permanent. They're meant to evolve. What once worked may no longer fit. What felt right in one season might hold you back in the next. That's not failure—it's a sign you're growing.

This week isn't about overhauling everything. It's about choosing one part of your day and shaping it with purpose. Start something that supports who you are now—or change something that no longer does.

Your future self doesn't need something perfect, just a pattern you've chosen with purpose.

Good Days Run on Routines

Every day is shaped by routine, whether you're aware of it or not.

How you start your morning. How you check email and move through meetings. What you do after the kids get home or go down for a nap. How you spend the hour after work. How you wind down before bed. These repeated patterns subtly shape how you feel, what you focus on, and how your day runs.

Some routines support you. Others slowly wear you down.

The issue isn't having routines—it's letting them form without intention. A routine you didn't choose can run your whole day on autopilot. And you may not notice it until you're stressed, distracted, or behind.

However, when you choose a routine intentionally, everything becomes easier. You make fewer decisions. You feel more grounded. You get energy back. That's the power of a good routine—it gives you structure that works for you, not against you.

Daily Routine

When looking to improve a routine, most people focus on what they want to do. But effective routines start by asking what you need. Do you need more focus? More ease? More recovery? A good routine meets that need without adding pressure.

Maybe your workday would run more smoothly if you checked email only at set times instead of reacting to every notification. Or perhaps you'd sleep better with a bedtime routine that included ten minutes of screen-free time to read or reflect.

You don't need a complete system. You just need one small routine that makes life easier—and helps you show up better.

The Fast Path to a Better or Changed Routine

1. Pick one part of your day that could work better.
Morning, afternoon, evening—it doesn't matter. Choose the time that feels most scattered, rushed, or reactive.

2. Decide what routine would improve that time.
Do you need more structure? More calm? More energy? Choose one small, repeatable pattern that would help, like planning tomorrow's priorities, prepping meals, blocking focused work time, or starting the day with a clear intention.

3. Anchor it to something you already do.
Tie it to an existing part of your day. After coffee. Before your commute. At your desk at midday. Right when the kids go to bed. Repetition is easier when the trigger is already there.

4. Do it daily this week. Track what shifts.
Don't aim for perfection. Just consistency. See how this one routine affects your focus, energy, or stress. Let results shape what comes next.

The Awareness Path to a Better or Changed Routine
Start noticing your default routines. What do your mornings look like? How do you usually spend your evenings? Are you choosing those patterns—or just falling into them? This week, pay attention to one routine you've outgrown. You don't

need to fix it all at once. Just bring awareness to what you're repeating and ask whether it's still serving you.

Your What If Action

This week I will _____

_____

_____

_____

_____

_____

_____

_____

_____

_____

_____

PAUSE. QUESTION. GO.

A Change & Growth Inflection Chapter

Years ago, I attended a personal development seminar. The speaker walked on stage, dimmed the lights, and clicked to his first slide. What appeared looked like the flight path of a confused flock of geese. Boxes. Arrows. Circles. Labels. More arrows. I felt a little motion sickness.

Then he proudly announced he was going to walk us through his fifteen-step process for creating personal transformation.

I almost burst out laughing. Not at him. He was clearly passionate. But at the absurdity. Who's going to remember and practice fifteen steps? Not me. In fact, the only steps I took that day were the twelve or so it took to slip out of the auditorium quietly.

He missed what most people miss: Personal change and growth must be simple enough to practice.

Science backs this up. Our brains process, recall, and respond better to things grouped in threes. Consider how frequently the number three appears in communication, decision-making, and design. There's even a term for it: the rule of three. It's why stories have a beginning, middle, and end. It's why we say, "Ready, set, go."

It's why the What If Rule uses three steps:

Pause. Question. Go.

They're not just a catchy sequence. They're a practice. And they're all actions.

PAUSE. Catch the moment. Break the pattern. Interrupt your autopilot.

QUESTION. Ask a What If question that gives you a better perspective or fresh options.

GO. Take one small step in that new direction.

Simple. Actionable. Repeatable.

That's also why the weekly What If chapters serve two purposes. Yes, each one is designed to spark real change that week. But each question is also an invitation to practice the What If Rule itself.

You're not just doing something different. You're building the habit of creating change. Over time, "Pause. Question. Go." becomes automatic.

It's how you discover new ideas and find better ways to do things. It becomes how you respond to stress. It's how you make better decisions. It's how you shift when stuck.

One What If question can change your week.

Practicing the What If Rule can change your life.

5.

WHAT IF THIS WEEK, YOU LIVE WITHOUT COMPARING YOURSELF TO OTHERS?

It's sneaky, isn't it?

You didn't wake up planning to compare. But somewhere between checking your phone and starting your day, it crept in.

You saw someone's Instagram post. Someone else's vacation, someone else's morning routine, someone else's highlight reel of a life.

Maybe it wasn't even intentional. A friend's promotion. A neighbor's remodel. A colleague's new project. You weren't looking to feel less than, but somehow, your solid day suddenly felt smaller.

That's how comparison works. It doesn't shout. It whispers. *You should be further along. You should be doing more. You're not enough.*

And just like that, your energy scatters. Your self-worth dips. You start second-guessing decisions that felt perfectly fine five minutes ago.

Research shows we naturally evaluate ourselves by comparing ourselves to others, especially when we feel uncertain. Your brain scans your environment to figure out where you stand. That worked fine when the village had twenty people. But now, your brain is comparing you to thousands of filtered highlight reels before you finish your first cup of coffee. No wonder it's exhausting.

But what if this week, you didn't play that game?

Meanwhile, on Planet Perfect

You know the place. Everyone is thriving, glowing, and living perfect family lives, building empires before breakfast, and never forgetting to stay hydrated. That's the fantasy world comparison invites you to visit. And it's exhausting.

Comparison is a thief not just of peace of mind but of presence, purpose, and possibility.

When you start measuring your life against someone else's, you stop seeing your own clearly. You lose track of what you value. Instead of asking what matters to you, you chase someone else's version of success.

The worst part? Half the time, you don't even want what they have. You just don't want to feel behind.

But there is no behind. There is only forward, from where you are, with what you have.

A friend of mine used to take his family camping. He would wander around the campgrounds looking at all the families having a wonderful time together and wish he had that. He could have, but he was away from his family, comparing what he saw others had.

That constant comparison kept him from enjoying what he had. His family was right there, ready to make memories with him. But he was so busy watching other families that he missed his own. He was living his life and missing it at the same time.

Dare to Not Compare

The fundamental shift begins when you catch comparison early. Instead of trying to shut it down with logic or guilt, pause and ask what story you've just told yourself. Is it about being behind, missing out, or not measuring up? Then ask if that story is even yours.

Most comparison pulls you toward someone else's path while disconnecting you from your own. It keeps you from seeing your progress and growth. But when you notice it happening and shift your focus back to what matters to you, you reclaim something far more valuable than status. You reclaim your direction.

The Fast Path from Comparison to Contentment

1. Identify your comparison trigger.

Who or what sets it off most often? A specific person on social media? A coworker? A friend's success story? Name it. You can't shift what you don't see.

2. Choose your redirect.

When you notice yourself comparing, what will you focus on instead? Maybe your progress this week. A goal you're working toward. Something you're grateful for. Decide now so you're ready.

3. Take one action toward your path.

Instead of watching someone else move forward, take a step

on your own. Make a call. Do the task. Write the thing. Let movement replace the spiral.

4. *Curate your inputs.*
If something consistently pulls you into comparison, mute it. Step back. You don't need to watch someone else's life to live your own.

The Awareness Path to Catching Comparison
Notice when comparison shows up and how it shifts your mood or momentum. Pay attention to the story it tells you— usually that you're behind or that you're not enough. Each time you catch it, you have a chance to choose something better: your own path, your own progress, your own definition of enough.

Your What If Action

This week I will

6.

WHAT IF THIS WEEK, YOU MADE THE DECISION YOU'VE BEEN POSTPONING?

Oprah Winfrey knew her news anchor job wasn't right for her. She often ignored the whispers that something wasn't right. She was afraid to let go, unsure of what was next. "Your life is always speaking to you. Sometimes it's in a whisper," she's said.

In time, the whispers got louder. She was reassigned from the anchor desk to a local talk show. At first, it felt like failure. But the moment she stepped into the new role, everything shifted.

"I knew instantly that this is what I was supposed to do."

Sometimes, the decision you've been postponing is the one that finally sets you free.

Here's what I've learned from years of coaching: The decisions we postpone aren't necessarily the biggest ones. They're the important ones that matter to us. The ones that will change how we feel about our days, our relationships, or our sense of direction.

The Decision That Won't Go Away

The decision sits there, waiting. It's been waiting for weeks, maybe even months. You think about it from time to time. Not every day, but it's always with you.

Maybe it's having that difficult conversation with your aging parent about their living situation. You know it needs to happen. You see the signs that they're struggling. But every time you start to bring it up, you find a reason to wait. Next visit. When things are calmer. When you have more time to talk.

You tell yourself you need more information. More time. A clearer sign. The perfect moment when all the uncertainty dissolves and the right choice becomes obvious.

But deep down, you already know what needs to happen. You just haven't decided to move forward.

Maybe this is the week you do.

Because the moment you decide, everything opens up. Not because the decision is perfect or because all the fear disappears but because you stop leaking energy into indecision and start channeling it into movement.

The Liberation of Choosing

Forward movement creates the clarity that thinking in circles never will. You adjust. You learn. You adapt. But from a standstill, all you can do is think in circles.

Every time you make a decision without perfect conditions, you build trust in yourself. You realize most decisions are flexible. Few are final. And even the wrong ones still move you forward.

When working with clients who have been indecisive about something, I guide them through three key questions:

1. What's the real decision you're avoiding? Not the surface-level one but the deeper shift it would represent.

2. What story are you telling yourself about what might happen if you choose wrong? Most fear isn't about the outcome—it's about identity risk.

3. What's the cost of staying undecided? Decisions drain us most when they sit unresolved. Meanwhile, we miss out on opportunities and growth.

Just walking through those questions often creates the clarity someone needs to move forward.

The Fast Path from Indecision to Action

1. Name the real decision.
Often, the question you're asking isn't the one you're facing. *Should I quit my job? might become Am I ready to bet on myself?* Get clear on the actual choice in front of you.

2. Set a decision deadline.
Give yourself a specific date. Maybe Friday, at the end of the weekend, or whatever feels fair but firm. Write it down. Say it out loud. Without a deadline, delay becomes the default.

3. Gather only what you need.
You don't need perfect information. You need enough to move forward. If you've been circling for a while, you probably already have it.

4. Choose forward movement.

When you're stuck between options, choose the one that stretches you—the one that pushes you closer to the life you want, not the one that keeps you safe.

The Awareness Path to Seeing Your Next Decision

Pay attention this week to what you keep circling back to. Notice the question that won't leave you alone. You don't have to act on it yet—just name it. Naming the real decision is often the first step toward making it a reality. The decision you've been postponing isn't waiting for the perfect moment. It's waiting for you to trust yourself enough to take the next step forward.

Your What If Action

This week I will _____

_____

_____

_____

_____

_____

7.

WHAT IF THIS WEEK, YOU GAVE YOURSELF CREDIT FOR WHAT YOU'RE DOING WELL?

Most people are better at noticing what they didn't do than what they did.

They'll say, "I could've done more" instead of "I handled that well."

They'll spot the flaws and skip right past the effort.

They'll give credit to everyone else but ignore their own contribution.

That's not just a personality quirk. It's how the brain works. Experts call it the negativity bias. Your brain pays more attention to what went wrong than what went right. It does that to protect you. However, if you're not careful, it can also train you to overlook your growth, effort, and successes. Which means you keep improving without ever feeling it.

And that's a problem. Because when you never acknowledge what you're doing well, you miss the chance to learn from it, build on it, and repeat it.

John was like that. He got things done. He showed up for people. He kept things moving forward. But he rarely gave himself credit. Every time something worked out, he brushed it off. He'd say it was luck. Or timing. Or that someone else would've done it better.

So he tried something different.

Each day, he paused to name one thing he'd done well and what made it work. At first, it felt awkward. But over time, something shifted. He started seeing patterns. His preparation, his tone, his timing—those weren't accidents. They were strengths. Real, repeatable strengths.

The more he named them, the more confident and grounded he became. Not because someone else validated him but because he finally began to notice what he was capable of.

Your Brain's Drama Department

The moments you're proud of. The way you handled a challenging situation. The effort you gave when you didn't feel like it. The calm you brought into a chaotic moment. Those aren't just feel-good highlights. They're coaching moments.

Noticing what you're doing well gives you something more powerful than praise: insight. You start to understand what's working, why it worked, and how you can build on it.

That's what self-coaching looks like. It's learning from your own experiences in real time. It's turning awareness into growth. It's noticing your wins, naming the choices behind them, and using that information to grow stronger and more effective.

Becoming Your Own Biggest Fan

You don't need someone else to tell you you're improving. You can see it for yourself. In recovery, it's referred to as a spot inventory. A quick review of what you just said or did. Do it without judgment.

I like to ask myself what I did well and what I can do even better. This way, I can give myself credit for a job well done and use it as a point of growth.

This isn't about ego or pretending everything is perfect. It's about recognizing that you're learning as you go. That's self-coaching. It changes everything and takes just a few minutes a day.

The Fast Path from Wins to Wisdom

1. Choose one moment each day when you did something well.
Perhaps you remained calm during a challenging moment. Solved a problem. Got something important done. Encouraged someone else. Pick one.

2. Ask some self-coaching questions.
What made it work? Was it how you prepared? How did you listen? How did you stay focused or follow through? Find the effort or quality behind the result.

3. Capture it in a sentence or two.
Write it down or say it out loud. "That worked because I stayed patient." "I helped because I stayed present." This locks in the lesson.

4. Use that insight going forward.
Once you know what works, it's easier to reach for it again. That's how progress compounds.

The Awareness Path to Recognizing Your Strengths

Start noticing how fast you move past your good moments. Do you tell yourself they don't count? That anyone could've done it? This week, pause long enough to see what you did right. Give yourself credit without minimizing it. Then ask: What made that possible, and how can I build on it?

Your What If Action

This week I will _____

_____

_____

_____

_____

_____

_____

_____

_____

_____

8.

WHAT IF THIS WEEK, YOU RUN WITH AN IDEA YOU'VE BEEN THINKING ABOUT?

Ever wonder why people sit on ideas instead of moving forward? There are usually three reasons: They're waiting for perfect conditions that never come; they're waiting for more time, money, or resources; or they're avoiding potential failure.

So the business idea stays in your head. The home renovation project gets postponed again. The creative pursuit waits for "when things slow down." The career change remains a someday plan.

You keep waiting for permission that's never coming and perfect conditions that don't exist.

Reid Hoffman spent years thinking about professional networking online. How it should work, what features it needed, and how professionals would connect. But when LinkedIn finally launched, he discovered the real value wasn't what he'd been planning for. Users started recruiting in ways he'd never imagined. The "people you may know" feature proved more valuable than the networking tools he had initially focused on.

All that time refining the concept in his head, he couldn't have predicted what would matter most to users. The platform's real value emerged from how millions of people used it in real situations. You just don't know until you take the next step.

Where Good Ideas Go to Hibernate

I often see this with the people I coach. They have brilliant ideas, genuine passions, and creative impulses that could change their lives or, at the very least, bring them joy. But they treat those ideas like they're too fragile to touch until everything is perfect.

Meanwhile, their time is spent on obligations and everyone else's priorities. The idea sits in the background, waiting for a mythical moment when life calms down and they finally feel ready.

But ideas don't improve by sitting in your head. They improve by moving forward.

Even a rough first step will teach you more than weeks of thinking. Once you start, unexpected momentum kicks in. You meet people. You uncover resources. You see opportunities you couldn't spot from the sidelines.

Every time you act on an idea, even if it's clumsy or messy, you prove something important: You're the kind of person who makes things real.

The Power of Messy Beginnings

Most people wait for clarity. But action is often what creates it.

When you run with an idea, even just a little, you start turning unknowns into information. You find out what excites you, what's harder than expected, and what opens up next.

That doesn't happen when ideas stay in your head.

The trick is to stop evaluating and start exploring. Treat your idea like something worth trying, not perfecting. The goal isn't to have it all figured out. The goal is to learn what's possible once you begin.

I have a friend who always seems to be involved in something new. I used to think he quit on too many things. Then I came to see he quit on more things than most people started. That also meant he saw more ideas through than most people. Something I took from him and applied to my life is that there's nothing wrong with Ready. *Go. Set.* Well, unless it's something that could cost you a significant amount of money or damage important relationships.

The Fast Path from Thinking to Doing

1. Pick one idea that keeps coming back to you.
Choose something that energizes you, not something you think you should do. It doesn't have to be big. It just has to be something you care about.

2. Identify a very doable first step.
Don't map out the whole plan. Choose one action you can take this week. Send an email. Buy a domain. Write a paragraph. Take one small, clear step.

3. Set a deadline for that first step.
Put it on your calendar. Allocate it real space in your schedule, just as you would for any other priority.

4. Focus on learning, not perfecting.

You're not building the final version. You're discovering what happens when you move. Every action teaches you something; planning alone never will.

The Awareness Path to Ideas That Keep Calling

This week, notice what idea keeps resurfacing. The one that still tugs at you. The one you mentally revisit when you have space to think. Ask the action question: What if this idea is ready now, not someday? You don't have to act on it today. Just stop dismissing it as a future project.

Your What If Action

This week I will _____

_____

_____

_____

_____

_____

_____

WHAT REAL CHANGE LOOKS LIKE

A Change & Growth Inflection Chapter

The most challenging part of my day once I quit drinking was always 5 p.m., when I'd lock up my store. Before I'd quit, that's when the party would begin every evening. In complete honesty, I'd already had a few drinks during the workday, but 5 p.m. was when things took off. It was the signal to go home, start drinking, and numb everything out.

But when I got sober, I'd still close the store at 5 p.m. and go home. Except now, I didn't drink. I just sat there. Uncomfortable. Restless. My brain was racing, and my chest was tight. I didn't know what to do with myself. I wasn't drinking. But I wasn't OK either.

Then someone gave me a simple but powerful suggestion: Make a change. Don't go straight home. Go to the park. Visit a friend. Drive around for a bit. Break the pattern.

It sounded too easy. But I tried it.

And it worked.

That's when I learned what real change looks like.

Most people think change is about big life decisions or sudden wake-up calls. But it's not. Change is when you do something different in a moment you usually wouldn't. That's it. Simple as that. That's where it starts.

It doesn't have to be dramatic. It doesn't even have to feel good right away. It just has to be different.

You interrupt the pattern. You shift the autopilot. You show yourself that a different path is possible. One moment like that can change the direction of a day. Stack enough of those days together and your life begins to change too.

Real change can look like someone who constantly checks work email at night deciding to turn their phone off during dinner. It can look like a parent who usually loses patience during homework time pausing, taking a breath, and trying a different approach. It can be the person who never speaks up in meetings deciding to share one idea anyway. It can be as simple as choosing not to eat at that particular fast-food place anymore.

None of those changes are massive on the surface. But they break patterns. They shift what was automatic into something intentional. Once you do that, you've already started to change.

And here's the thing. One day, I realized I could go home at 5 p.m. again. I didn't dread it. I didn't avoid it. It felt normal.

Not because the hour changed but because I had.

9.

WHAT IF THIS WEEK, YOU LET YOURSELF FEEL WHAT YOU FEEL WITHOUT JUDGING YOURSELF?

One of the most challenging aspects of running a company was having to lay off employees. It never got easier. The business I led was closely tied to interest rates and demand, so staffing levels fluctuated in response to market conditions. When I hired them, I always warned people about the volatility. But that never made it easier when the time came.

Hiring people was fun. Letting them go was awful. I never lost sight of what it meant for them. They weren't just losing a job; they were also facing financial fear and uncertainty, having to job search again, explain what happened, and pick themselves back up. During those meetings, many people broke down and cried. Some apologized for it. A few even got frustrated with themselves for crying at all.

I always made sure they knew their reactions were valid. That it was OK to feel what they were feeling, right there in front of me. Half the time, I was crying too. And I never judged myself for it.

Somewhere along the way, many of us learned to second-guess our emotions. We were told to be strong. To stop crying. To toughen up. To get over it already. We started to believe that feeling sad, overwhelmed, anxious, or even just off meant something was wrong with us.

But what if that's not true? What if your feelings aren't flaws to fix but rather signals to acknowledge?

You don't have to be consumed by your emotions to honor them. You don't have to let them run the show. But judging yourself for feeling them adds a second layer of pain that's entirely optional.

This week's What If question is simple: What happens when you stop labeling your emotions as wrong, weak, or overdramatic and just let yourself feel them without self-criticism?

The Emotional Police

Many people carry a quiet shame for how they feel. They think they're too sensitive. Or too emotional. Or not emotional enough. They believe they should have moved on by now. Or that someone else would be handling it better.

I heard about someone who said to his wife, after she had experienced something deeply painful, "It's time to get over it." He wasn't being cruel. He just didn't know how to hold space for her pain. But in saying that, he sent a clear message: Your grief is making me uncomfortable, and I think you should be done now.

This happens all the time. Not always out loud but in glances. In rushed check-ins. In the way we talk to ourselves. And especially in how we talk to kids. Somewhere along the way, we absorb the idea that big feelings are problems to fix, not part of being human.

The Permission to Feel

When you push feelings down or away instead of acknowledging them, it usually backfires. It increases stress and prolongs the feelings. But when you permit yourself to feel without labeling it as wrong or weak, you create space for clarity, healing, and even strength.

This doesn't mean acting on every feeling. It doesn't mean wallowing. And it certainly doesn't mean endorsing harmful thoughts or impulses. You can feel something and still choose how to respond.

It's also important to understand the difference between self-pity and self-empathy. Self-pity keeps you stuck and centers on helplessness. Self-empathy moves you forward. It says, "This is hard, and I still deserve care."

When you let yourself feel without judgment, you're not giving in to weakness—you're choosing self-empathy, and that's strength in motion.

The Fast Path to Emotional Permission

1. Name what you feel.

Don't overanalyze. Just name it. *I feel sad. I feel numb. I feel angry. I feel off.* You don't need a reason for it to be real.

2. Notice any judgment.

Are you telling yourself you shouldn't feel that way? Is it too much? Does that mean something is wrong with you? Spot the inner critic.

3. Comfort and support yourself.
Say, "It's OK to feel this. I don't have to fix it right now. I'm allowed to feel what I feel."

4. Let the feeling move.
Feelings pass more easily when we stop holding on to them. Breathe. Walk. Talk to someone safe. Write it down. Give it motion instead of shame.

The Awareness Path to Feeling Without Judgment
At some point this week, you might feel something rise— sadness, frustration, loneliness, or anxiety. When it does, pause and ask yourself: *What if this isn't wrong? What if this feeling just needs space rather than fixing?* Give it five minutes of honest acknowledgment before you try to move on. That's not weakness. That's emotional strength without the judgment.

Your What If Action

This week I will

10.

WHAT IF THIS WEEK, YOU REPRIORI-TIZED SOMEONE YOU CARE ABOUT?

This question is dedicated to my mother, Aura Fleener.

There's usually someone we've been meaning to get in touch with. They cross our minds regularly, but something always comes up—work deadlines, household tasks, the daily rush. We tell ourselves we'll reach out this weekend, but the weekend fills up with errands and obligations.

Your college roommate or an old coworker sends the occasional text, and you respond. But it's been months since you've had a real conversation. You miss it, but coordinating feels complicated. You'll figure it out soon.

The problem isn't that you don't care. It's that you've made them more optional in a life that's full of demands.

In my case, it was my mother.

The Lesson I Learned Too Late
When my mother was alive, I called her regularly. But not as often as I could have. I was raising a family and growing a business. She understood. She never complained. She was always glad to hear from me. Which made it easy to assume

there would always be a next time. Another call. Another week.

After she passed, I realized I should have made those calls a higher priority. Not because our relationship was broken but because time with the people we love is never guaranteed. And it is definitely finite.

It made me think of Harry Chapin's song "Cat's in the Cradle." The father is always too busy. Always pushing connection off for later. And when later finally comes, the moment is gone.

The people who love you most are often the ones who get the least of your time, because they're the most understanding about not getting it. They wait. They're patient. And sometimes, they wait too long.

The Urgent Versus Important Trap

It happens at different stages of life. Something urgent always seems to crowd out something important. The deadline feels more pressing than the relationship because it has visible consequences. The person you love will understand. So they wait.

We tell ourselves that next week will be calmer. After this season, this project, this stretch, we'll have more time. But the pace never slows. It just changes shape.

Staying in touch has also changed. A quick text feels like staying connected. A like on social media seems like a gesture. But those digital nudges don't create the kind of connection that truly matters.

When People Come First

Here's what I've come to learn, and what I hope you realize sooner than I did: When you put people first, everything else still gets done. The work adjusts. The calendar stretches. Most of the things that seemed urgent were never urgent. They were just noisy.

Relationships don't need hours of time or the perfect setting. They need attention. A fifteen-minute call means more than a perfectly planned visit that never happens. A commute is a great time to reconnect. So is a walk. So is now.

Some people avoid reaching out because it's been too long, and they feel guilty. Others are so focused on doing and achieving that they don't realize who they've unintentionally pushed to the margins.

If you're someone who keeps meaning to connect but never gets around to it, you're likely prioritizing what's loud over what's lasting. If you're someone who avoids the call because it feels awkward or overdue, the delay only makes that more challenging.

Either way, the outcome is the same—disconnection, even from people you care about deeply.

Reprioritizing someone isn't just for their benefit. It reconnects you to what matters. It softens stress. It grounds you in something more profound than deadlines. And often, it gives you exactly what you didn't know you were missing.

The Fast Path to Prioritizing People Who Matter

1. Pick one person who matters to you but isn't getting the priority they deserve.

Spend a little time with this. Who have you been meaning to reach out to but keep pushing aside? Start with one.

2. Schedule time with them this week, just like any other important commitment.
Put it on your calendar. Don't wait for time to appear. Make it. Do it right now.

3. Make the time together all about them.
Don't lead with how long it's been or how busy you are. Ask about their life. Show up fully. Turn off the alerts. Close the laptop. Be present.

4. Decide how often you want to connect and set the next time now.
Don't leave it to chance. If this person matters enough to prioritize once, they matter enough to prioritize again.

The Awareness Path to Catching Relationship Drift
Take note this week of who you keep saying you'll reach out to. Notice who crosses your mind but never quite makes it onto your calendar. That's your signal. Not to feel guilty but to take one step toward reconnection. The urgent things will always be loud. But the people you love won't always wait.

Your What If Action

This week I will _____

_____

_____

11.

WHAT IF THIS WEEK, YOU UPDATED A STORY YOU TELL YOURSELF?

We all carry narratives about who we are. Some of them serve us well. They help us feel grounded, motivated, and capable. But others were formed during moments of stress, failure, or fear, and we've carried them far longer than they deserve.

A manager who had a few difficult conversations that went poorly decides they can't hold people accountable. A person who burns dinner a few times in college declares themselves a bad cook. Someone who has had a couple of difficult relationships believes they will never find a lasting relationship.

These stories feel like facts because we've repeated them for so long. But they're just conclusions we drew from limited data during moments when we were learning, tired, or caught off guard.

A failed presentation becomes "I'm terrible at public speaking." A financial mistake becomes "I'm bad with money." One fender bender becomes "I'm an unlucky driver."

What makes these stories so powerful is how they shape our choices. If you believe you're not a people person, you avoid networking and leadership roles. If you think you're not creative, you don't try new approaches or share new ideas.

Most of these beliefs were formed when we had less experience, fewer tools, or different circumstances. But we carry them forward as if they are fixed truths about who we are.

The Stories That Stick Around Too Long

These internal narratives help us make sense of life, but they're not always accurate. Sometimes they lock us into a version of ourselves we've long since outgrown.

The most liberating realization is that these aren't facts. They're just stories. And stories can be rewritten.

Psychologists have a term for this: narrative identity. It's how we organize our experiences into a coherent sense of who we are. These stories can be powerful tools for growth, but they can also become invisible barriers that limit what we think is possible.

David Versus the Computer (Spoiler: David Wins)

David believed he wasn't tech savvy. He typed slowly. Avoided new tools. When something on his computer glitched, he felt stuck. Over time, this became his story: "I'm not a tech person."

So when a department head position opened up that required using project management software and coordinating digital tools across the team, David didn't apply. He told himself the role needed someone more naturally skilled with technology. A younger colleague with less experience got the job.

Months later, tired of always feeling behind and missing opportunities, David decided to stop avoiding technology. He started watching short tutorials. He asked a teammate to show him how the project system worked. He practiced.

Bit by bit, things began to make sense. He realized he wasn't incapable. He had just never given himself permission to learn.

When a similar position came up again, David applied. In the interview, he didn't pretend to be an expert. He talked about the skills he had developed and how he had overcome the story he used to believe.

He got the job. Later, he admitted the technology had never been the real barrier—the story had been.

Spotting the Stories You've Outgrown

Most limiting stories don't sound dramatic. They appear in everyday self-talk and subtle explanations. You hear them in what you believe you're not good at, not wired for, or not meant to do.

One way to surface them is to ask, *What would I try if I didn't already believe I wasn't good at it?* That question pulls the story into the light. You don't have to rewrite it yet. But once you see it, you can start to challenge whether it still deserves to shape your future.

The Fast Path from Old Story to New Truth

1. Identify one story you tell yourself that limits what you attempt.
Pick something specific—"I'm not good with money," "I can't lead a team," "I'm not creative." Choose a story that keeps showing up in your decisions.

2. Trace the story back to where it started.
When did you first decide this was true about you? What event or feedback planted that idea? Often, it's based on limited or outdated experience.

3. Look for evidence that contradicts the story.

Find moments where you've done better than you give yourself credit for. What's always been there but didn't fit the story?

4. Catch yourself when the story starts and reframe it.

When you notice yourself thinking, *I'm not good at . . .*, stop and shift it. Say, "I'm learning how to . . ." or "I haven't figured this out yet." The goal isn't to fake confidence. It's to stop reinforcing a version of you that no longer fits.

The Awareness Path to Hearing Your Self-Talk

This week, notice the labels you casually assign yourself. Listen for when you say, "I'm just the kind of person who . . ." and ask where that belief came from. You don't have to rewrite the story yet. Just notice which stories might no longer be true.

Your What If Action

This week I will _____

_____

_____

_____

_____

_____

12.

WHAT IF THIS WEEK, YOU FOUND STRENGTH IN A DIFFICULT MOMENT?

Anderson Cooper, in his podcast *All There Is,* shares stories about grief that are raw, personal, and unexpectedly grounding. After the death of his brother and later his father, he described feeling hollowed out, like life was moving on without him. But in those days when even getting out of bed was a victory, he experienced moments that broke through the heaviness. A stranger's kindness. A laugh that caught him off guard. What stayed with me was how he helped me see that grief and strength aren't opposites. You don't have to wait until the pain ends to find resilience. Sometimes, you find it because of the pain.

That idea of finding strength in the middle of something difficult, not just after, is what this week's What If is about. It doesn't have to be something dramatic. It could be a week where everything feels heavy. When work is overwhelming. When someone you love is struggling. When your motivation disappears, or maybe when you're just not having a good day but can't quite explain why.

A few years ago, I was diagnosed with prostate cancer. The news came through my health app just as I was boarding a red-eye flight. I remember seeing the word cancer as we taxied down the runway. Even knowing that it's often curable, I was scared. But as the plane lifted into the night sky, I felt something unexpected—a strange calm. Maybe it was being closer to God. Or perhaps something else. But in that moment, I found a kind of strength that surprised me.

The Strength You Don't Notice

Most people think strength is about pushing through. But real strength often shows up quietly. It's in the breath you take before answering a hard question. The restraint not to snap back when you're overwhelmed. The way you keep moving, even when you don't feel ready.

We often don't notice those moments as a strength. But they are. They're not loud or dramatic, but they matter. And you usually don't realize how strong you are until you look back and see what you made it through.

If you're going through something hard right now, whether it's grief, uncertainty, a health scare, or a loss, this chapter isn't about powering through or finding a silver lining. It's about noticing that even here, in the thick of it, you're still showing up. You might not feel strong. You might feel tired, numb, angry, or afraid. And still, you're carrying something heavy and moving through your day.

This isn't about pretending you're OK. It's about recognizing the small signs of resilience that often go unnoticed. The text you sent. The shower you took. The moment you let yourself cry. Those things count. That's strength too.

When Strength Doesn't Feel Strong

It's common to assume that if you're crying, anxious, or overwhelmed, you must not be strong. But psychologists who study stress-related growth have found something different. People often experience surprising resilience and personal growth not after the difficult moment is over but during it.

That strength might look like:

- Asking for help
- Sharing with someone that you're struggling or scared
- Getting out of bed when it would be easier to stay in it
- Letting yourself feel something fully instead of stuffing it down

You don't have to feel strong to be strong. Strength isn't a feeling. It's often just choosing the next right step in the middle of uncertainty.

The Fast Path to Finding Your Hidden Strength

1. Name the difficult moment.

What are you carrying this week? Don't compare it to someone else's situation. Just name it. Grief, disappointment, anxiety, a relationship strain. Whatever it is, acknowledging it gives you clarity.

2. Look for one sign of strength.

It could be small. You made a phone call. You stayed calm when you wanted to panic. You paused before reacting. Find a moment when you did something hard without calling it heroic.

3. Support your capacity.

What's one thing you can do to make the next hard moment easier? Is it asking for help? Taking a break? Putting your phone down? This isn't about being tougher. It's about supporting your strength.

4. Let the strength count.

Don't dismiss it. Don't say, "Well, that was nothing." Let it matter. Give yourself credit for how you're handling something difficult. That's how internal resilience grows.

The Awareness Path to Recognizing Resilience

There may be a moment this week when you feel uncertain, tired, or emotionally stretched. In that exact moment, pause and ask yourself: *What strength am I showing right now that I'm not giving myself credit for?* Sometimes the most powerful thing you can do is simply notice that you're still here, still trying, still showing up. That's resilience in action, even when it doesn't feel heroic.

Your What If Action

This week I will _____

_____

_____

_____

13.

WHAT IF THIS WEEK, YOU EMBRACED SOMETHING ABOUT YOURSELF?

I dropped out of college in my sophomore year. I was working full-time, partying full-time, and going to school full-time. Something had to give. It wasn't the best choice I ever made.

I was always self-conscious about dropping out. It never held me back in the companies where I worked, but it still bothered me. There was always this nagging feeling that I was somehow incomplete, like I was missing something everyone else had. At times, I felt less than others.

Twenty-five years later, when my speaking and coaching business had taken off, I decided to return to college to complete what I had started. I was going to get that degree and finally feel legitimate.

I enrolled in evening classes. One night, I was sitting in an accounting class, learning things I already knew and had been doing successfully for years. The professor was explaining theories I had figured out through experience. That's when it hit me. I didn't need the degree.

I was there because some part of me believed I needed it to feel whole, to feel worthy, to feel enough. What I needed instead was to embrace the part of me that had taken a different path. I was spending time and money trying to validate my past instead of building my future.

I walked out of that class and never went back. Not because education isn't valuable but because I finally understood that I needed to accept and embrace the decision I had made. I was no better or worse because of it.

Your Internal Wrestling Match

We all have parts of ourselves we resist, hide, or try to change. It might be something from your past—a decision you made, a path you didn't take, or an experience that shaped you. Perhaps it's something about your personality. You're too quiet, too loud, too emotional, too analytical.

It could be physical. Your height, voice, age, or appearance. Or circumstantial. Your background, family, financial situation, or education level.

We spend enormous energy trying to hide these things, compensate for them, or fix them. We apologize for who we are instead of owning it. We make decisions based on shame or embarrassment rather than strength.

When You Stop Wrestling and Start Winning

Embracing yourself starts by accepting that you are who you are—no more wrestling with it. You are right where your feet are. No judgment. No shame, apology, or guilt. Just looking forward.

For me, embracing my nontraditional education meant I could focus on growing my expertise through experience rather than chasing a credential to prove something. It freed up the energy I had been using to explain or justify myself.

For others, embracing their lack of formal education might mean choosing to pursue further learning. The key is that you cannot make good decisions from a place of shame or denial.

You move forward based on where you want to go, not what you're trying to hide or fix about where you've been.

You may discover that the very things you once saw as weaknesses are what make you valuable. Your unconventional path may be what makes you relatable. Your sensitivity may be what makes you a great leader. Your background may be what helps you connect with people others can't reach.

Embrace what is true, and you'll move forward as your authentic self.

The Fast Path to Self-Acceptance

1. Identify one thing about yourself you've been fighting, hiding, or trying to change.

Choose something specific that drains your energy. Something you apologize for, avoid, or try to downplay.

2. Consider what embracing this would look like.

How would your thinking or behavior shift if you stopped resisting this part of yourself? How might you show up differently if you owned it?

3. Take one action this week that comes from embracing rather than hiding.

Make a choice that reflects who you are, not who you think you're supposed to be. Let this part of you guide, rather than limit, your decisions.

4. No more apologizing for it.
Accept it as part of your story and a testament to your strength. Make peace with it and move from that place.

The Awareness Path to Embracing Yourself
Notice how often you resist something about yourself. Is there a moment when you shrink back or second-guess because of your past, your personality, or your circumstances? When you feel the urge to hide or explain, pause and ask the embrace question: What if I embraced this instead? What would I do differently right now?

Your What If Action

This week I will _____

_____

_____

_____

_____

_____

_____

_____

_____

WHAT REAL GROWTH LOOKS LIKE

A Change & Growth Inflection Chapter

I used to think growth would feel like standing on top of a mountain with my arms stretched out, wind in my hair, and a motivational quote below me. You know the poster.

But most of the real growth in my life hasn't felt anything like that. It's looked more like doing the same thing I've always done but choosing to do it just a little better. Or doing something differently for the third day in a row, even when nobody notices.

Growth is rarely dramatic in the moment. It's quieter than that. Sometimes it feels boring. Sometimes it feels like nothing's happening. But that doesn't mean it isn't working.

We tend to notice growth only in hindsight. We look back and realize, *I didn't react like I used to*. Or, *I didn't run from that situation. I stepped in*. That's growth. And it didn't come from a breakthrough. It came from practice.

Intentional growth is different from forced growth. Forced growth occurs when life presents a significant challenge and you have no choice but to adapt to it. We all experience that. But the most meaningful growth often happens when you decide to grow—on purpose. That's when you build something more substantial, not just something that survives.

Intentional growth is a daily decision. It's showing up with a little more awareness. A little more discipline. A bit more grace. Not every day will feel like a win, but when you keep practicing, you're growing even when you can't see it.

Then one day, you respond with calm instead of frustration. You stay present when you would've checked out. You don't avoid the hard conversation. You make the call, say the thing, take the next step.

That's growth.

And if you keep going—if you keep choosing small, intentional steps forward—those quiet choices will stack up. One day, you'll look back and realize you're standing on a mountaintop. Not because you sprinted there but because you climbed deliberately and consistently.

It all starts with asking a different kind of question.

What if I tried something new this time?

What if I tried a different approach?

That's the beginning of real change and growth. And that's the power of What If.

14.

WHAT IF THIS WEEK, YOU SAID NO TO SOMETHING YOU'D USUALLY SAY YES TO?

The request comes in. A calendar invite hits your inbox. A project lands on your desk with the word *urgent* attached. Someone at home assumes you'll handle it because you always do. You're the first person the school asks for help.

And before you've even thought about it, you hear yourself saying yes.

Not because you want to. Not because it fits your priorities. Just because it feels easier than saying no. Or because saying yes has become automatic.

Until later, when the regret sets in. When the time you didn't have gets used up. When the resentment creeps in.

The Automatic Yes Trap

It's common to say yes before you've even thought about what you're agreeing to. Sometimes it's out of habit. Sometimes it's the fear of disappointing someone. Sometimes it's tied to your identity—you've always been the one who handles things.

But the fundamental shift starts when you separate your

impulse from your intention. You don't need to justify your no. You just need to believe you're allowed to have one. When your yes is always automatic, your time and priorities stop being your own.

I Can't Believe I Just Said Yes Again!

A former colleague of mine should have come to work dressed in a cape. She was Superwoman. She worked an extremely high number of hours. She volunteered for every project. And she had three kids in elementary school, where she was heavily involved in their classrooms.

I was in awe of how much she did. Then one day, after she raised her hand for yet another project, we were walking out of the meeting when she muttered, "I can't believe I just said yes, again." That caught me off guard.

We talked about it later. She admitted she was tired, stressed, and maxed out. Behind her constant yes was someone who desperately needed permission to say no.

Saying yes to something you don't want to do doesn't just drain you—it also undermines your self-worth. When you say yes from a place of pressure or resentment, it shows. In your tone. In how you show up. In the energy you bring—or don't bring—to the work. You're not doing anyone a favor by agreeing to something half-heartedly.

From Reflex to Choice

I have a personal rule: I don't say yes unless I can mean it. That doesn't mean I only do things I love. But it does mean I don't agree to do something and then resent it. If I need to adjust my mindset to get there, I will. But I won't fake a yes just to avoid discomfort.

The more honest you are with your yes, the more trustworthy it becomes. People know you'll show up fully. And you begin to spend your time in ways that reflect your actual values, not just your people-pleasing reflex.

This week is about noticing the automatic yes pattern and choosing differently, on purpose, not out of pressure. You can keep the cape. Saying no when you used to say yes is, in fact, a superpower.

The Fast Path to Intentional Choices

1. Practice the pause.
Allow yourself time to consider before responding to requests. Try saying, "Let me check my calendar" or "Let me think about that" to break the automatic yes cycle.

2. Get to an authentic yes or an honest no.
If your reaction is hesitation or dread, ask what would make the request feel more comfortable. Could the timing change? Could you help in a smaller way? Or do you need to say no altogether?

3. Practice your no language.
Decide ahead of time how you'll decline. Try saying, "I can't take that on right now" or "That doesn't fit with my current priorities." Having language ready makes it easier to respond clearly and kindly.

4. Offer a helpful redirect if needed.

If you can't say yes, guide the person to another option. Suggest a different solution, timeline, or contact. You're still being helpful, just not at the expense of your priorities.

The Awareness Path to Breaking the Yes Reflex

Notice this week when you're about to say yes, before you've given it a thought. What's driving it? Is it guilt, habit, or pressure to be the dependable one? Start to question that reflex. Your time and energy deserve a real choice, not just an automatic response.

Your What If Action

This week I will _____

_____

_____

_____

_____

_____

_____

_____

_____

15.

WHAT IF THIS WEEK, YOU ELIMINATED ONE THING THAT DRAINS YOUR ENERGY?

For eight years, Sarah organized the monthly group meeting. She reserved the room, made the coffee, arranged the chairs, and stayed to clean up. She started when the group was small and needed someone reliable.

But her life changed. She had two young kids and a demanding job. The monthly meetings became a source of stress instead of service. She'd come home exhausted, short with her family, and quietly resentful of the time it took.

The group had grown to over thirty people. It was thriving. But Sarah couldn't bring herself to stop. No one else was volunteering.

Of course they weren't. She was still doing it.

Finally, she realized her reliability had trapped her. What began as meaningful had become draining. She announced she'd be stepping down in two months and offered to train whoever wanted to take over. Three people volunteered immediately. The group didn't fall apart. It continued to thrive, and Sarah got her evenings back.

Sarah learned how energy is finite, how every yes to something that drains you is a no to something that could energize you.

The Energy Vampire Club

We tend to think of energy drains as minor frustrations. Just part of being a responsible adult or being dependable.

But they not only make you tired. They slowly drain your presence, your patience, and your ability to show up for what matters.

And the trickiest part? Most energy drains don't appear to be problems. They look like loyalty. Generosity. Responsibility.

Energy drains come in different forms. Some are commitments that no longer fit your life. Some are relationships that have shifted over time. Others are habits or routines you've outgrown.

The key is recognizing that not all drains require you to walk away completely. Sometimes you can address them directly and change how they work.

When You Don't Have to Walk Away

I know someone who had a childhood friend she still talked to regularly. They'd known each other for over forty years. But lately, every call left her feeling worse. Her friend had become consumed with politics, and the conversations turned into long rants about what was wrong with the world.

Instead of ending the friendship, she had an honest conversation. She told her friend that the calls had shifted and left her feeling drained. She wasn't accusing—she was just sharing how she felt.

She suggested they focus more on their families, shared memories, and what was happening in their actual lives rather than getting pulled into political frustrations every time they talked.

The friend was defensive at first. But then she softened. She agreed to try. And now their calls feel better, for both of them.

That's the thing about energy drains. You don't always have to eliminate them. Sometimes, you just have to name them, address them, and adjust your relationship with them.

Permission to Let Go

The hardest part isn't identifying what drains you; it's recognizing what you can do about it. It's permitting yourself to change it. Most people wait for permission from someone else or for things to blow up before they're forced to let go.

But change doesn't require crisis. It requires clarity.

You're allowed to shift a routine that no longer fits. You're allowed to adjust boundaries, even if they've been in place for years. You're allowed to step back from commitments that have become more burden than blessing—not to abandon responsibility but to release the version of it that's quietly costing you more than it gives.

The Fast Path from Energy Drain to Energy Gain

1. Identify what consistently drains you.

Pay attention this week to what leaves you feeling depleted. What do you dread? What do you do out of obligation rather than choice?

2. Challenge the "should."
Ask yourself: *Am I doing this because it adds value to my life, or because I think I should? Because I want to, or because I'm afraid of disappointing someone?*

3. Calculate the real cost.
What could you do with that time and energy instead? What are you saying no to by continuing to say yes to something that drains you?

4. Take one action to eliminate or shift it.
Cancel the subscription. Resign from the committee. Have the conversation. Set a boundary. Say no to the next request. You don't need to fix every energy drain. Just start with one.

The Awareness Path to Recognizing What Drains You
This week, take note of what consistently drains your energy. Some things you might be able to address right away. Others might need more thought or planning. Start with awareness, but don't hesitate to take action when the opportunity arises.

Your What If Action

This week I will _____

_____

_____

16.

WHAT IF THIS WEEK, YOU LET GO OF REGRETTING SOMETHING FROM YOUR PAST?

I woke up on a plane to Dallas with no memory of how I got there and a pocketful of cash. It was the last money from a family business I'd destroyed with my cocaine habit. I was a twenty-eight-year-old addict and thief who had hit absolute rock bottom.

When I got home, my father had discovered I'd been stealing for years. Meeting with him was worse than waking up on that plane.

In recovery, I learned that I couldn't move forward while regretting what I'd done. The constant replaying and wishing it had been different was not making me a better person. It kept me stuck in the identity of someone who steals, lies, and ruins things.

As long as I defined myself by my worst moments, I couldn't become someone different.

Letting go of regret wasn't saying what I did was OK. It was releasing myself from a past I couldn't change, so I could focus on a future I still could.

The Regret Replay Channel

Regret comes in all sizes. Some regrets are massive, like ending a relationship, walking away from an opportunity, or hurting someone you care about.

Others seem smaller but still linger. Saying the wrong thing in a conversation, not speaking up when you should have, or making a very public mistake at work. Just because it's not dramatic doesn't mean it hasn't been weighing on you.

Big or small, the only way to move forward is to stop carrying it backward.

When Your Brain Gets Stuck in Reverse

When you can't stop regretting something, your brain gets caught in a loop. You replay the same scenario. You wish for different outcomes. You dissect every move, hoping you'll find something new.

It feels like learning. But it's just reliving.

Your brain loops regret because it's trying to solve something that already happened. That's the trap. Guilt can be useful—it points you toward repair. But rumination just replays the pain without a purpose.

Regret starts to shape your identity. You don't just remember what happened. You become it. You start seeing yourself as someone who messes things up. And when that becomes your filter, you act accordingly. You overexplain. You hesitate. You assume people see the worst version of you, even when they don't.

Most painfully, you stop learning from what happened because you're too busy feeling bad about it. The lesson gets buried under shame.

The Art of Letting Go

Letting go of regret isn't the same as forgetting. And it's definitely not about excusing what happened. It's about choosing not to hold it against yourself forever.

Many people think regret means they're staying accountable. But living in regret doesn't mean you're taking responsibility. It often means you're stuck in self-punishment.

What helps is reflection, not repetition. The turning point usually comes when someone realizes they've learned from the experience but haven't let that learning change how they see themselves.

You don't need to pretend it didn't happen. You just need to drop it so it's no longer the headline of who you are.

The Fast Path from Regret to Release

1. Acknowledge what happened without minimizing or dramatizing it.

Name it honestly. No excuses. No exaggeration. Just clarity about what happened and who you were at the time.

2. Make amends where possible, then stop.

If a repair or apology is needed, do it. But don't stay stuck trying to undo what can't be undone. Some regrets aren't meant to be fixed—they're meant to be released.

3. Take the lesson and apply it.

What did you learn? What would you do differently? What red flags would you catch sooner now? A mistake becomes useful the moment it helps you make better decisions.

4. Do something to bury the regret.

Write it down on paper, then tear it up or burn it. Say it out loud, then let it go. Create your way of closing that chapter—something simple, but real. A small ritual that says, "I'm done carrying this."

The Awareness Path to Spotting Regret

Notice this week where your thoughts still loop back to regret. Ask whether you're replaying for growth or just punishing yourself. Pay attention to how carrying regret affects your energy and confidence. Most people don't realize how much mental space regret takes up until they start letting it go. Forgiveness doesn't erase the past. It frees you to move beyond it.

Your What If Action

This week I will

17.

WHAT IF THIS WEEK, YOU DIDN'T LET SOMEONE'S BAD MOOD OR NEGATIVITY AFFECT YOU?

We all know someone like Eeyore.

Not mean. Not trying to ruin anyone's day. Just . . . Eeyore. A little gloomy. A little grumbly. Low energy. Low vibe. Not especially interested in looking on the bright side.

And if you've ever watched how Winnie the Pooh handles it, there's a quiet lesson in emotional boundaries.

Pooh doesn't argue with Eeyore. He doesn't try to cheer Eeyore up or fix their mood. He doesn't catch the gloom like a cold and start sulking too. He just stays Pooh—curious, kind, and primarily focused on honey. He invites Eeyore along but doesn't get pulled into the fog.

What if we approached the real-life Eeyores in our lives the same way?

The Pooh Method

The reality is, you're going to cross paths with people who are off, negative, or in a funk. At work. At home. Online. In the grocery store parking lot. You don't have to judge them for it.

You don't have to fix them. And you don't have to join them.

The most important thing you can do in these moments is to protect your energy without punishing theirs. That doesn't mean shutting down or walking away. It means being aware and noticing when someone's mood is starting to influence yours, and making a choice.

The choice to stay grounded, lead with curiosity instead of judgment, and stay connected without being consumed.

The moment you notice your thoughts shifting—getting annoyed, defensive, or pulled into their mood vortex—that's your signal. That's your chance to reset. You can take a breath, step back internally, and remind yourself: *This is theirs, not mine.*

You're not ignoring them. You're not dismissing their experience. You're simply refusing to hand over your emotional remote control.

Which Way Are You Moving?

I live my life with the idea that at any moment, I am either moving toward or away from peace and happiness. Some interactions lift you. Others drain you. When someone else's energy pulls you off course, you get to decide whether to follow it or to shift back toward your center gently.

There's also a surprising upside to these moments. When you practice emotional boundaries like this, you don't just avoid unnecessary stress. You build trust in yourself. You learn that peace isn't something others give or take away. It's something you protect. And every time you stay rooted in your mindset, you make that peace a little easier to return to next time.

Most people who get pulled into someone else's negativity

don't realize it until they're already in it. The key is to catch it early. You'll feel it in your body first—tight shoulders, shallow breathing, the urge to snap or retreat. That's the moment to pause, name what's happening, and gently return to your center. You don't need to match their mood to stay present.

The Fast Path to Emotional Boundaries

1. Catch the energy early.
Not the words but the weight. Notice when a conversation or mood starts to pull you off center.

2. Shift your attention.
Instead of focusing on their mood, bring your focus back to your own center.

3. Decide what you want to bring.
You don't have to match the moment. Ask yourself: *What tone do I want to set right now?*

4. Let them have their weather.
Every person walks under their own sky. You don't need to carry an umbrella for clouds that aren't yours.

The Awareness Path to Protecting Your Energy

Notice when someone else's mood starts to shift yours. Pay attention to the physical signs first—tension, shallow breathing, that urge to react. You can't control other people's moods, but you can control how much space they take up in your head. When you practice staying grounded in the presence of negativity, you build emotional endurance and protect the peace you've worked hard to create.

Your What If Action

This week I will _____

_____

_____

_____

_____

_____

_____

_____

_____

_____

_____

_____

_____

YOUR THINKING FOLLOWS THE DOING

A Change & Growth Inflection Chapter

One of the hardest things I've had to admit in my life is that I was a quitter.

I had quit school. Quit relationships. Quit jobs. Almost everything—except for the things I should have quit.

And what hurt most was that it wasn't always dramatic. It was quiet quitting, slowly pulling away and letting things fade instead of following through. I hated that about myself, but I didn't know how to change it. I had all the right thoughts, all the self-awareness, all the reasons to be different. But none of it ever stuck.

Then I heard someone say something that flipped the entire script.

"You don't think your way into a new way of acting. You act your way into a new way of thinking."

That was it. That was the thing I'd been missing. I didn't need to wait until I had the right mindset. I didn't need to wake up with unshakable confidence. I didn't have to fix my past before I took a step forward.

I just had to act.

So I did. I stopped trying to become someone who didn't quit. I just kept showing up. When it got uncomfortable, I stayed with it. When I wanted to escape, I didn't. I kept going even when it felt awkward, even when my mind told me I couldn't.

And little by little, something started to change. The more I took action, the more my thinking followed. I wasn't trying to force change anymore. I was living it.

That principle changed everything for me. And now I see it everywhere. People try to think their way into motivation. Think their way into confidence. Think their way into discipline.

It rarely works that way.

Real change almost always starts with doing. Take the action first. Your mindset will catch up.

18.

WHAT IF THIS WEEK, YOU FOUND A BETTER WAY TO SPEAK YOUR MIND?

For most of my life, I avoided confrontation. I grew up seeing disagreement as arguing, and I hated arguing. Ironically, I never actually argued much. I just avoided hard conversations altogether, especially at home. I convinced myself I was keeping the peace, but really, I was bottling things up until they exploded over something small.

At work, I didn't have this problem. I could speak clearly and directly without getting emotional. But in personal relationships, I didn't know how to have a challenging conversation without it feeling like a fight.

My wife, Joanna, helped me improve in this area. Early in our relationship, she could tell when something was bothering me. Instead of letting it fester, she'd gently say, "Just talk to me." It wasn't always easy, but I slowly learned that speaking up in the moment prevented things from escalating into something bigger. It made space for honesty and closeness. Not conflict.

Some people hold things in, like I used to. Others let it fly and say what they think in the moment, even if it comes out too hot. Most of us do a little of both, depending on the situation.

But either way, the real skill is learning how to speak up in a way that builds connection, not tension.

If you recognize these patterns, this week is about finding a better way.

The Goldilocks Zone of Speaking Up

Avoiding hard conversations creates distance. Rushing into them with frustration creates defensiveness. The opportunity lies in noticing your pattern and shifting it just slightly.

Speaking your mind isn't about winning; it's about being true to yourself. It's about being clear, kind, and connected. Whether you need to be more honest or more thoughtful, this week is about choosing a better way to communicate.

At work, this shows up in two common ways. You either avoid bringing up issues with coworkers or your manager, or you deliver feedback too bluntly, risking damage to trust. The key is preparation and intention.

If you tend to hold back, schedule a quick check-in and lead with curiosity. Try something like, "I wanted to get your thoughts on how we handled that project," instead of letting resentment build if you're often too direct. Pause before sending that email. Ask yourself: *How can I say this in a way that builds clarity and collaboration?* Think through your main point and lead with what you want to accomplish together rather than focusing on what went wrong.

When It Gets Personal

Family conversations can be emotionally charged, especially with children or close relatives. With kids, it can be easy to overreact or lecture instead of calmly addressing the situation.

With parents or siblings, we often fall into old communication habits that don't serve anyone.

Try replacing reaction with reflection. Instead of raising your voice, ask a question: "Help me understand what happened here." Instead of shutting down, share how something made you feel: "When you said that, it hurt my feelings." With family members who push your buttons, pause and remember you're talking to someone you love, not someone you need to defeat. These small shifts can lower the emotional temperature and open up a more meaningful exchange.

The Fast Path to Connected Communication

1. Name your default style.
Do you tend to hold it in or let it out too quickly? Get honest about your usual pattern.

2. Catch the moment early.
Notice when something bothers you or feels off. Pause before you react or retreat.

3. Choose a better starting point.
If you hold things in, start by asking, "Can I share something with you?" If you speak too fast, try saying, "Give me a moment to think about how to say this."

4. Focus on connection, not correction.
Speak your truth but stay curious. Aim to understand, not just be understood.

The Awareness Path to Your Communication Style

This week, pay attention to your communication patterns. Do you feel your chest tighten when you need to speak up? Do you find yourself rehearsing conversations in your head instead of having them? Or do you notice yourself speaking before you've thought through how to say something? Watch for the moments when you either retreat or rush in, and ask yourself: *What would it look like to stay present, grounded, and honest without letting fear or frustration take over?*

Your What If Action

This week I will _____

_____

_____

_____

_____

_____

_____

_____

_____

19.

WHAT IF THIS WEEK, YOU STEPPED INTO ANY FEELINGS OF BEING OVERWHELMED?

A few years ago, I kept saying I was overwhelmed. My calendar was packed. My inbox overflowed. Everything felt urgent. But what I eventually realized was that I wasn't just overwhelmed. I was overloaded.

Overwhelm is the feeling. Overload is the reality of having too much on your plate.

Most of us don't choose to be overloaded. It just happens. Work ramps up. Family needs grow. Someone leaves, and now you're covering for two. Life gets lifey, and before you know it, you're stretched too thin.

You may not have chosen the load, but you do get to choose how it plays out.

That's what I had to own. I wasn't setting limits. I wasn't protecting my energy. I was saying yes to everything and resenting it all. And I kept treating being overwhelmed like a personal flaw instead of a flashing light on the dashboard.

You can't change what you don't own. So this week, what if you stepped into that feeling, not to sit in it but to work with it?

Your Internal Alarm System

When people feel overwhelmed, they usually point to what's around them. The schedule. The workload. The demanding boss. The demanding kids. The never-ending to-do list. And often, they're right. The pressure is real, and the load really is too much.

Here's what most people miss: Overwhelm is a form of feedback. It's your internal system telling you that something needs to shift before everything else starts to suffer.

That's why taking a step into it matters. Not to fix everything at once but to listen to what it's trying to tell you. Where are you stretched too thin? What boundaries are missing? What could you put down, even temporarily?

The mistake most people make is trying to power through overwhelm instead of pausing to understand it. They think the solution is to work harder, move faster, or just push until it passes. But overwhelm doesn't usually resolve itself. It escalates until something forces a change—burnout, a mistake, or a breakdown.

When Everything Feels Urgent

I know someone who described her overwhelm perfectly: "It feels like I'm playing a game where every ball in the air is made of glass, and I can't let any of them drop." That's the trap of overwhelm—everything starts to feel equally important and equally urgent.

Not everything that feels urgent actually is. When you're overwhelmed, your brain starts treating every task like an emergency. The work email feels as urgent as picking up your kid. The grocery shopping feels as critical as the project deadline.

Taking a step into overwhelm means getting honest about what's actually urgent versus what just feels that way. It means asking: If I could only handle three things today, what would they be? That simple question can cut through the mental noise and help you see clearly again.

And it means giving yourself permission to handle things differently. Ask someone to help, or delegate if possible. Skip the grocery store and just order something. Let the laundry wait another day. Send a quick text instead of a long email. Not everything has to be done your way or done perfectly. Sometimes, good enough is exactly enough.

The Fast Path to Understanding Your Load

1. Name the overload clearly.
Have you taken on too much? What are you pretending is fine when it's not? Say it clearly to yourself. No need to sugarcoat it.

2. Feel it fully instead of fighting it.
Don't push through or pretend it's not there. Sit with the overwhelm for a moment. Let yourself acknowledge how much you're actually carrying without immediately jumping to solutions.

3. Take one thing off the table.
Pick one thing you can cancel, delay, delegate, or simply let go. Lighten your load without guilt. One small release can shift everything.

4. Choose recovery, not just relief.

Relief is distraction. Recovery is restoration. This week, choose one thing that restores you: sleep, movement, solitude, laughter, or whatever fills your tank.

The Awareness Path to Working with Overwhelm

This week, when overwhelm hits—the tension, the scattered feeling, the sense that everything is urgent—pause instead of pushing through. Ask yourself: *What am I actually carrying right now? What's mine to handle, and what isn't?* That moment of honest assessment is where your power lives. You can't change what you won't acknowledge.

Your What If Action

This week I will

20.

WHAT IF THIS WEEK, YOU CELEBRATED SOMEONE OR SOMETHING JUST BECAUSE?

When I was running a retail store years ago, I had a thought that stuck with me: Why do we wait to celebrate people until they leave?

Think about it. Someone gives years of their time, energy, and effort, and the celebration happens when they walk out the door. That's when we order the cake and say the kind things we've probably thought for years.

So one day, I decided to flip it. When a new employee started, we had a cake. We put up a sign that read "Welcome. You're going to be great here." We didn't wait for a milestone. We made their first day a celebration.

That moment didn't just make them feel good. It shifted the energy of the whole team. People smiled more. Laughed more. Everyone got excited about welcoming a new person. They started looking for ways to support the new hire. It changed the tone of the day because celebration is contagious.

Celebrate, Come On!

(I hope you sang that last line. Thank you, Kool & The Gang.)

We all want to feel seen. And we all have the power to create that feeling for someone else.

Most people think good things about others but rarely say them out loud. *She's really holding things together. He's been showing up in a big way lately.* Those thoughts stay trapped in our heads.

Celebration is how we bridge that gap. It's a moment that says, "I noticed." And it matters.

This isn't about throwing a party or going over the top, although that is fine. This is about naming and honoring something good, just because you can.

When we celebrate someone else, they feel valued. It lights them up. But it does something for us too. It lifts our energy. It reminds us of what's good, what's working, and what's worth appreciating. And it has a ripple effect. People nearby pick up on it. They feel it. They often pass it on.

That's the power of unexpected celebration. It creates a connection and gives everyone a shot of meaning.

The Art of Random Celebration

Celebration is usually tied to a specific event. A birthday. A milestone. A goal hit. But what if it wasn't about the event? What if it was more about a specific person or feeling?

Maybe someone made your day easier. Maybe they've been quietly showing up in ways you've noticed but never named. Choosing to celebrate that moment, without needing a reason, can shift how you both feel.

You're not waiting for something big. You're simply honoring what's already there.

The Fast Path to Spreading Joy

1. Look around and find someone in your life who deserves a moment of appreciation or recognition.
Not for a big win. Just for who they are or what they've been showing up for.

2. Pick a day and time, then decide how you will celebrate them.
A note. A post. A cake. A text. An email blast. Take them out to coffee or a meal.

3. If you'd like, make it playful and create your own award or moment.
Best Daughter Ever. Friend Who Shows Up. Calm in the Chaos. Kindness Ninja. Make it yours.

4. Observe what it creates for them and the impact on those around them.
Notice how they respond. Pay attention to the energy it adds to the moment, to you, and to anyone nearby. Small celebrations can quietly lift an entire environment.

The Awareness Path to Noticing the Good
This week, notice the good you see in others and how often it stays in your head. What might happen if you let it out? What might change if you celebrated out loud, just because you can?

Your What If Action

This week I will _____

_____

_____

_____

_____

_____

_____

_____

_____

_____

_____

_____

_____

_____

_____

21.

WHAT IF THIS WEEK, YOU PUSHED THROUGH ONE EXCUSE IN THE MOMENT IT SHOWED UP?

I pulled into the driveway and saw my neighbor struggling to unload something heavy from his car. I thought about going over to help, but the excuses came quickly.

I'm tired.
He'll be fine.
He's younger.
He probably doesn't want help anyway.

I walked inside.

But from the window, I could still see him. Still struggling. Still alone. The excuses were right there, ready to wrap things up for me. And for a second, I considered letting them.

Then I didn't.

I went outside, walked over, and asked if he needed a hand. He said he was fine. Of course he did. That would've been the perfect moment to turn back.

Instead, I stayed, and we completed the task in under five

minutes. No big deal to him, probably. But it was a shift for me.

Because that moment wasn't about being helpful; it was about pushing through the excuse before it won.

Your Brain's Best Excuse Generator

Most people believe that excuses are a sign of weakness or a flaw. They're not. They're built-in protection systems. Excuses are our brain's way of keeping us safe and comfortable. When something feels uncertain, the brain offers an excuse to protect you from discomfort, rejection, or failure.

I'm too tired.
It probably won't matter.
I'm too busy to help.
This isn't the right time.
They might say no.

And most of the time, we don't even recognize them as excuses. We just believe them.

But every excuse arrives with a window. A moment where you can pause and say, "Not this time." A moment where a new response becomes possible.

The Moment You Can Push Through

The excuse isn't the problem. Believing it without question is.

That's what this week is really about—not eliminating all excuses forever. Many are valid. But even valid excuses deserve a second look.

That's how you turn hesitation into motion. And how motion

creates better moments.

Most people try to overcome excuses by digging deeper into motivation. You don't need to feel ready or convinced. You just need to recognize the excuse for what it is and ask a better question.

Try asking, "What's the right next thing?"

Not the perfect thing. Not the easiest thing. The right thing, for you and for the situation. Sometimes the answer is to help. Sometimes it's to rest. If I had been exhausted, then maybe the right thing would have been not to help him, for his sake and mine.

The goal isn't to blindly push through everything. It's to pause long enough to make a considerate choice instead of a default one.

The Fast Path to Breaking Through

1. Name the excuse when you hear it.
Even silently saying there's an excuse can change your response.

2. When you hear it, pause and ask yourself: *What's the right next thing here?*
Not the easiest thing. Not the perfect thing. Just the next right move.

3. Do something small in that direction.
It doesn't have to be bold. Just something that moves you forward before the excuse takes over.

4. What did you learn as a result?
Maybe you learned the excuse wasn't as valid as it felt. Maybe

you proved to yourself that momentum is still possible, even in a small moment.

The Awareness Path to Moving Forward

This week, don't try to eliminate your excuses. Just notice them. Especially the ones that sound most reasonable. You might find that pushing through a single excuse opens up more than a single result. It opens up momentum.

Your What If Action

This week I will _____

_____

_____

_____

_____

_____

_____

_____

IT'S NOT A STRAIGHT LINE

A Change & Growth Inflection Chapter

There's a regular comic strip called *The Family Circus*. Years ago, I saw one in which the mom said something like, "Billy, come straight home." Then the next panel showed a dotted line tracing Billy's exact path through a neighbor's yard, across a fence, behind a tree, over a playground, and finally back home. Not exactly a straight line.

That comic strip stuck with me. Not just because it was funny and charming, but because it's exactly how real-life growth looks.

We're told to "stick to the plan." We expect ourselves to move in a straight line—start here, finish there, no detours. But that's rarely how it goes. Even when we're focused, intentional, and committed, the path zigzags. Life gets in the way. We slip back into old habits. We hit moments of doubt. And sometimes we just wander off course for a while.

That doesn't mean we've failed. It means we're human.

I can't count how many times I've looked back at a period and realized I was making more progress than I thought I was. Not because I crushed every goal or followed a flawless routine but because I kept coming back to the path—even if I'd taken a long, meandering detour first.

Change and growth often feel like circling the same lessons

more than once. You don't just learn something and never forget it. You return to it again and again, each time with a little more clarity, a little more strength, a bit more self-awareness.

That's not failure. That's integration.

You don't need to go in a straight line. You just need to keep going.

There's value in the long way. There's growth in the detours. There's wisdom in every loop and bend and pause, as long as you keep stepping forward when it matters.

So when things don't go perfectly, that's OK. If you fall into an old habit, lose momentum, or drift for a while, it doesn't erase your progress. It's just part of your dotted-line path. What matters is that you keep coming back to what matters. That you keep moving.

Because even the winding path still gets you home.

22.

WHAT IF THIS WEEK, YOU PRACTICED BEING A LITTLE HAPPIER?

Some people seem to radiate happiness, even when things aren't going their way. And let's be honest: Most people don't trust it. You've probably heard (or said) something like "Nobody can be that happy all the time." The assumption is that they must be faking it, delusional, or in denial about how hard life is.

But the genuinely happy people I've met aren't pretending everything is perfect. They've simply discovered something most people haven't: You can be happier, even in the middle of life's messes.

At a speaking engagement, I had lunch with an attendee, and we ended up talking about happiness. He shared that he had recently lost a significant contract and had to scale back his team. "It was brutal," he said.

But even during the stress and hard conversations, he made time to stop by his favorite bakery on the way to the factory. He also sent notes of appreciation to the people who stayed with him. "I can't change what happened," he told me, "but I can still choose how I feel going forward." That line stayed with me. I came to see it as what I now call the Happier Way.

It's not about chasing constant joy or ignoring pain. It's about owning your role in how you experience your day. Not just reacting to life but shaping your mindset and behavior in ways that support being a little happier. On purpose.

This isn't positive thinking. It's conscious living. It's understanding that happiness isn't the result of external conditions falling into place. It's the result of inner choices—attention, intention, and action—all of which are within your control.

Taking Back Your Remote Control

The shift begins when you stop waiting for happiness to show up and start seeing it as something you can create.

This isn't about forcing yourself to feel good all the time or pretending things are fine when they're not. It's about finding a little light even when things are hard and not feeling guilty for doing so.

Of course, there are real barriers that can make happiness feel out of reach. Depression. Grief. Chronic stress. Trauma. In those situations, choosing happier means noticing moments when a slight upward shift is possible. And if it's not this week, that's OK too. The point isn't to pressure yourself into happiness. It's to remember you still have some agency, even when things are hard.

When You Stop Outsourcing Joy

Choosing happier doesn't mean ignoring what's hard. It means deciding that hard things don't get complete control of your emotional state. It means looking for lighter moments in a heavy day and choosing connection when it would be easier to isolate. Smiling at someone for no reason and creating joy in small ways, instead of waiting for circumstances to deliver it.

Most people say they want to be happy. But few people realize that they're outsourcing it. They hand their happiness to other people, unpredictable events, or external markers of success. That's why even when something good happens, the feeling doesn't always stick.

When you start to own your happiness, you reclaim it. You realize that being a little happier isn't a reward. It's a practice. And the more you practice, the more natural it becomes.

The Fast Path to Choosing Happier

1. Choose one moment to pause and redirect.
When something frustrates you this week, pause and ask yourself: *Is there a happier way to respond to this?* It might be letting it go. It might be laughing. It might be choosing calm instead of tension.

2. Create a micro-moment of joy.
Don't wait for the perfect day. Find or create one small moment—a song, a text to a friend, a good cup of coffee— that lifts you, even a little.

3. Protect your emotional space.
Being happier doesn't mean being available to everything and everyone. Say no when needed. Step away from the energy that drains you. Permit yourself to reset.

4. Acknowledge when you feel good.
Most people skip this part. But noticing when you feel even a

little better reinforces the habit. Say it to yourself: "This feels good. I like this moment."

The Awareness Path to Small Happiness Choices

This week, notice when you automatically let something steal your good mood. Pay attention to how quickly you hand over your emotional state to traffic, a rude comment, or a slight disappointment. In those moments, ask yourself: *What if I could still choose to be a little happier right now?* You're not ignoring what's hard—you're just refusing to let it control everything. That's the Happier Way.

Your What If Action

This week I will

23.

WHAT IF THIS WEEK, YOU CAUGHT YOURSELF BLAMING AND LET IT GO?

One morning, while writing this book, I got up before my wife. Her coffee is usually set to brew on a timer, but I was up earlier than usual, so I decided to swap in my coffee instead. We drink two different kinds of coffee, so I have to change to a different pot. A few minutes later, she came downstairs. I made her coffee too, but I forgot to switch the pot back.

Which meant when I brewed hers, it went into the pot that had mine in it. Now, both coffees were ruined.

And without hesitation, my mind turned to blame.

She should have gotten up when she usually does. I wouldn't have had to switch anything. Honestly, this is kind of her fault.

Then a half second later, I caught it.

It wasn't her fault. It wasn't even a big deal. I just made a simple mistake.

That's it—no one to blame. And really, no biggie.

That phrase, "no biggie," comes from Joanna when she was teaching special education. One of her students would get upset over small mistakes—a dropped pencil, a wrong answer, forgetting something at home. So Joanna started saying "no biggie" whenever these moments happened.

Eventually, the student began saying it too. Then the whole class picked it up. And I've come to love it. Because when you say it, you feel it. You realize how many things in life are only heavy because we carry them that way.

Your Brain's Favorite Scapegoat

Blame is a reflex. It happens fast, often before we're even aware of it. And it's not because we're careless or selfish. It's because our brain is trying to protect us.

When something goes wrong, your mind wants to shield your self-image. If you see yourself as responsible or thoughtful, then making a mistake feels like a threat to that identity. So your brain subtly shifts the cause outward.

Psychologists refer to this as the fundamental attribution error. We explain our behavior by the situation. But we explain other people's behavior by their personality.

I was late because traffic was terrible.

He was late because he's always disorganized.

See how that works?

What Dropping Blame Actually Does

Blame helps us feel in control. But in doing so, it often obscures the truth—and with it, the chance to reset, take a breath, and move on.

What made that coffee moment better wasn't fixing the mess. It was dropping the blame. As soon as I did, the whole thing felt lighter. I even laughed about it.

We don't need to carry the weight of every minor mistake. We don't need to keep assigning responsibility like we're running a courtroom. Sometimes the most helpful response is the simplest one: "no biggie."

Letting go of blame doesn't just help the people around you—it frees you up. It lowers tension. It diffuses frustration. It makes small things feel small again. And over time, it builds emotional freedom. You stop getting stuck in loops of resentment or irritation. You stop wasting energy assigning fault. You get to move on faster.

Most people think blame is about accountability. However, it's often more about self-preservation. When you catch yourself shifting blame, especially in small ways, it's a signal to pause. Not to shame yourself but to take back your power.

Letting go of blame isn't avoiding responsibility. It's choosing freedom over friction.

The Fast Path to Dropping Blame

1. Start with the small stuff.
Notice when blame begins to creep in during low-stakes situations—a delay, a mess, a misunderstanding.

2. Ask yourself the blame question.
Is this someone else's fault, or is this just a moment that didn't go as planned?

3. Consider "no biggie" as your reset phrase.
When you catch yourself blaming, say it out loud or in your head. Then congratulate yourself for seeing it. Or choose your own pivot phrase.

4. When someone is actually at fault, focus on solutions, not stories.

Blame may be accurate, but dwelling on it doesn't help. Shift from fault to forward motion. What needs to happen next?

The Awareness Path to Catching Blame

This week, simply notice how often blame shows up in your thoughts or conversations. You don't have to fix anything or change everything at once. Observe how blame feels in your body and mind when it arises. Even small blame carries weight. And letting go of it, even once, can make everything around you feel a little easier.

Your What If Action

This week I will _____

_____

_____

_____

_____

_____

24.

WHAT IF THIS WEEK, YOU MADE ONE CHANGE THAT YOUR BODY OR MIND WILL THANK YOU FOR?

Most people wake up with some version of the same promise: I've got to start taking better care of myself.

Drink more water. Go to bed earlier. Take an actual lunch break. Move your body. Go to the gym rather than just paying for it. Put your phone down before bed.

The things that might help aren't usually a mystery. But knowing and doing are two different things.

I get it. I've done it too. Mostly because I thought I had to change everything all at once.

Only 137 Steps and 18 Weeks to a New You

Most people approach health like they're prepping for a complete life makeover. Lose thirty pounds. Work out five times a week. Meal prep. Meditate. Hydrate. Sleep eight hours. All starting Monday.

By Wednesday, they're exhausted. By Friday, it's over. And on Monday, the whole cycle starts again.

I went through my version of this. I was feeling off—low

energy, poor sleep, just dragging through the day. I kept telling myself I needed a total reset. Eat better. Sleep better. Exercise. Cut stress. Fix everything.

But just thinking about changing everything at once made me procrastinate even more. That's the all-or-nothing trap. When the change feels too big, we delay it or give up the moment we slip.

So I asked a better question: What's one small change I can make this week that my body will thank me for?

The answer was simple. Go to bed thirty minutes earlier.

Within a few days, everything shifted. More energy. Better mood. Clearer thinking. That one decision didn't fix everything, but it changed how I felt every day. And it reminded me that momentum doesn't come from a total reset. It comes from a single move forward.

The One-Thing Revolution

Real change doesn't come from intensity. It comes from consistency. One meaningful, manageable shift can do more than a full reset you can't maintain.

When you choose something small that feels achievable and has a near-term benefit, your body and mind respond quickly. Research shows this creates what scientists call a "success spiral"—one small win makes the next change feel more possible. You feel the difference. That creates momentum, and momentum keeps you moving forward.

The secret isn't finding the perfect change. It's finding one you'll actually do. Something that feels so manageable you can't talk yourself out of it. Something that makes you feel better fast enough to want to keep going.

The Fast Path to One Healthy Change

1. Identify one specific change.
Not "get healthier" but "drink water instead of soda at lunch." Not "manage stress" but "take two short walks during the day." Make it specific and clear.

2. Make it small.
Pick something you know you can do. If it feels too big, make it smaller. You can scale later.

3. Focus on reduction, not elimination.
Instead of "quit coffee," try "one less cup." Instead of "no sugar," try "skip dessert during the week." Your brain is more willing to try something flexible.

4. Pick something with an immediate payoff.
Choose a change that makes you feel better quickly. Sleep, energy, mood. When you notice the benefit, it's easier to keep going.

The Awareness Path to Listening Within
Notice what your body or mind has been quietly asking for. Is it rest, movement, better food, or more space? You don't have to change everything. But this week, give that signal your attention. One small change can shift how you feel every day.

Your What If Action

This week I will

25.

WHAT IF THIS WEEK, YOU MADE SURE SOMEONE IN YOUR LIFE FELT TRULY SEEN AND HEARD?

One day, I was in a Starbucks when I noticed a dad and his daughter sitting a few tables over. She looked to be maybe nine or ten. They weren't fighting. Nothing was wrong. But something was missing.

She was talking. He was nodding occasionally. But his eyes were on his phone. Checking email. Scrolling. Glancing around. Half there. She didn't seem upset. She wasn't being dramatic. But I watched her slowly go quieter. Less expressive. Less animated. She didn't stop talking, but she stopped trying.

The dad probably didn't notice. He was doing what most of us do. He was juggling tasks, squeezing in time, being physically present while mentally somewhere else. And she probably didn't have the words for it. But in that moment, she wasn't being seen. And she wasn't being heard.

He missed it. Not because he didn't care but because he didn't realize the moment he was in. And that's the point. Most people don't feel unseen or unheard because someone doesn't love them. They feel it because that love, interest, or appreciation isn't being shown. And most of us don't realize we're doing it.

The Invisible People Right in Front of You

We've all been on both sides of this. Perhaps you've worked hard, but no one noticed. You've shared something meaningful, and someone changed the subject. You've walked into a room, or a meeting, or a moment, and felt invisible.

And most likely, you've also missed someone else's moment. Not because you meant to. Because you were tired. Distracted. Thinking three steps ahead. Or because they didn't say anything, and you didn't realize how much they needed to feel noticed.

The people who are most at risk of not feeling seen or heard are often the ones closest to us. The ones we live with. Work with. Talk to every day. The people who consistently show up, do the work, and handle what needs to be done. They're easy to overlook—not because they don't matter but because they rarely ask to be noticed.

At work, it's the person who shares thoughtful ideas in meetings but never gets a follow-up question. It's the one who delivers results but gets passed over in recognition because they don't self-promote. It's the quiet glue of the team—reliable, steady, and slowly beginning to wonder if anyone sees what they carry.

At home, it's the partner who handles the details and logistics without ever turning it into a headline. It's the child who doesn't interrupt and doesn't always get attention. It's the person who listens well but rarely feels listened to.

Most people don't need dramatic gestures. They're hoping

for presence. A moment of full attention. A look in the eye. A thoughtful question. Something simple—but meaningful enough to make them feel real again.

The Gift of Being Present

Being seen and heard isn't about volume. It's about presence. About paying close attention to what's often quiet and subtle and easy to miss.

We rarely intend to make someone feel invisible. It just happens. We're busy. We're distracted. Or we assume they're fine because they're not complaining.

But the people around us notice the gap. Even if they never mention it. And over time, they may stop sharing, stop showing up fully, or stop believing their presence matters.

If you're someone who's constantly juggling tasks, this is your reminder to pause and make eye contact. To give someone your full attention for just a few moments. If you're someone who assumes the people you care about already know how you feel, this is your chance to say it. To reflect something you see in them that they may not even see in themselves.

When you help someone feel seen, you strengthen them. When you help someone feel heard, you affirm them. And when you do both, you create the kind of connection that builds trust, safety, and lasting influence.

One of my favorite things is when, after talking with someone, one or both of us say thank you. Not for anything specific. Just for the shared moment. That is truly a gift.

The Fast Path to Making Someone Feel Seen

1. Pick one person to focus on this week.
Choose someone close to you—at work or at home—who might not be getting your full attention.

2. Give them some extra time for complete presence.
Put down your phone. Turn away from your screen. Look them in the eye. Listen without rushing to respond.

3. Reflect something meaningful back to them.
Name what you've noticed: "You've been handling a lot lately and doing it with such grace." "I see how much you care about this project." Say something they might not realize they needed to hear.

4. Make it a daily routine.
Build it in. Check in regularly. Ask one more question than you usually would. Let them know they matter without needing to be loud about it.

The Awareness Path to Noticing Who's Overlooked
Who around you might be feeling unseen, not because of neglect but because of routine or distraction? This week, pay attention to the quiet moments when someone is sharing something with you. Ask the presence question: *Am I really here, or am I just physically here?* What would change in your relationships if the quiet, steady people in your life felt truly acknowledged?

Your What If Action

This week I will

26.

WHAT IF THIS WEEK, YOU LET GO OF SOMETHING THAT ISN'T YOURS TO CONTROL?

Like many people, I was a fixer.

You had a problem? I had a solution. If I looked at myself honestly, I'd have to admit that I wanted to fix things so we could move on, especially in relationships. The quicker we solved an issue, the quicker the tension went away. For me, anyway.

The problem was that if the other person didn't want help or didn't listen to my advice, I'd end up feeling frustrated. Not just with the situation but with them. That only made things worse. What started as me trying to help turned into me carrying something that didn't even belong to me.

Then one day, I realized I was stepping into something that wasn't mine. I needed to stop and ask: What's theirs, and what's mine?

That question changed everything. Instead of offering unsolicited solutions, I started asking, "What can I do?"

That question lets me show up without taking over. It allows me to offer support while still respecting the other person's role and responsibility.

Psychologists refer to this as your locus of control—your sense of what is within your power and what isn't. When you try to control too much, it leads to frustration and burnout.

Letting go of what's not yours moves you back to clarity and peace. It's also central to acceptance and commitment therapy, which teaches that the way forward is often about allowing, not forcing.

That's Theirs. Not Mine.

For more than twenty years, I've used one simple phrase to keep myself from holding on to things that don't belong to me:

That's theirs, not mine.

It reminds me to pause, check, and sort.

When something frustrates you, throws you off, or makes you want to fix it, ask yourself: *What's theirs? What's mine?*

If it's yours—own it.

If it's theirs—release it.

This works even better when you make it physical. Picture the issue on a table between you and the other person. Can you pick it up? Move it? Change it? If not, it probably isn't yours.

Most people don't want to be passive. They want to stay engaged. But letting go isn't checking out. It's choosing where to stay in.

Letting go isn't apathy. It's clarity.

Where You Get Your Juice

You can't control whether your friend responds to your message today.

But you can control whether you spend your evening stewing

about it.

You can't control whether a coworker shows up grumpy again.

But you can decide not to take it personally or not to match their mood.

You can't control how a family member reacts to something you said.

But you can choose whether to keep trying to manage their emotions.

Sometimes, we don't realize we're holding on to an emotional hope. We want someone to treat us a certain way. To support us as we would support them. To respond with kindness, appreciation, or care. But if that's not who they are or something they're capable of giving, it creates a quiet frustration that builds up over time.

It's like trying to get orange juice from an onion. You'll only get onion juice. And the more you squeeze, the more disappointed you'll feel. Letting go in these moments doesn't mean giving up on people. It means accepting what they can't give you so you can stop trying to get it. That tastes a lot better.

On the flip side, you can follow up if something's unclear.

You can calmly reset expectations.

You can walk away, take a breath, or focus on something else.

Letting go doesn't mean you don't care.

It means you care enough to stay focused on what's yours.

The Fast Path to Letting Go

1. *Be aware when something grabs your mental energy.*
It could be a comment, a shift in someone's mood, or a problem you didn't cause, but suddenly, it's taking up space in your head.

2. Ask yourself: *What's theirs? What's mine?*
This is the moment to sort. If you can't act on it, influence it, or change it, it's not yours to carry.

3. *Decide on the next step.*
If it's not yours, let it go. If it is, take one small step forward. Either way, you're making a choice, not reacting by default.

4. *Refocus on what you can do.*
Ask yourself, *What's the right next thing for me?* That's where your clarity and momentum come from.

The Awareness Path to Letting Go
This week, when you feel yourself getting pulled into something emotionally, pause. Ask yourself if you're stepping into something that isn't yours. The more you practice that check, the easier it becomes to stay steady—and stay out of what doesn't belong to you.

Your What If Action

This week I will _____

BE EVEN BETTER

A Change & Growth Inflection Chapter

When I first started coaching people as a manager, I could never figure out why my employees resisted feedback. I was trying to help them improve their job performance. Make more money. Be more successful.

Then one day, it clicked.

I was giving feedback to someone who kept pushing back. Almost argumentative. They said they weren't doing anything wrong. I agreed. I told them I wasn't saying they were doing a bad job. I was just trying to help them be even better.

And bingo. That was it.

When I said they could do or be better, what they heard was that I was being critical because I thought they weren't good enough. So they defended themselves. They shut down.

That's when I realized I had to reframe my approach to growth and change. And it was easy. I started talking about how they could be even better. And it worked. Suddenly, people were listening and leaning in. Open to change. Open to growth.

To me, that's the real essence of growth—striving to be even better. It's forward-looking. It's without judgment. When we offer that to others, they respond. And when we offer it to ourselves, we do too.

That mindset became a foundational part of my personal development. Every day, I start with the decision to be even better than yesterday. Nothing dramatic. No pressure to transform everything. Just a daily effort to grow.

Over a week, a month, a year—that adds up. And not just incrementally. It builds. It expands. It compounds. You may not see the shift at first, but you'll feel it. And one day you'll realize that all the time you were just trying to be even better . . . you became someone extraordinary.

27.

WHAT IF THIS WEEK, YOU DIDN'T RESPOND WHEN YOU FELT COMPELLED TO?

Rich had a difficult relationship with his son. Every conversation seemed to turn into an argument. Every disagreement became a conflict. Over time, I noticed something simple but powerful—nearly every issue in their relationship came from the fact that each had to respond to everything the other said.

His son would make a comment. Rich would immediately feel the need to challenge it. His son would respond defensively, and Rich would fire back. Back and forth they'd go, each reply making things worse.

I reminded Rich that it takes two people to argue. If one person stops engaging, the argument comes to an end.

Eventually, my friend committed to stop responding just because he felt the urge. He still cared. He still showed up. But he stopped reacting to every comment. He no longer felt responsible for correcting every opinion or having the last word.

Not only did the dynamic shift but something unexpected happened—his son also started responding less. When one person breaks the cycle, the pattern ends.

The Compulsive Responders Club

Some people feel compelled to respond to everything. Every email gets a reply. Every meeting comment gets their input. Every conversation feels incomplete without their perspective.

I once worked with someone like this. She replied to every message. Spoke in every meeting. Often, she simply echoed what others had already said. Over time, people began tuning her out.

She didn't realize it. After I brought it up, she asked her sister if it was something she had always done. Her sister replied, "Oh yes, since you were a little girl."

No one had ever told her. They just stopped listening.

This habit isn't about ego. It's often about discomfort with silence, or the belief that silence means agreement or weakness. But silence can also signal confidence, restraint, and strength.

The Three-Question Test

In emotionally charged moments, the urge to respond quickly is strong. But fast reactions often create more noise than clarity. Before you speak, post, or reply, try this simple filter:

Does this need to be said? Many things do not require a response. Silence often speaks louder than words.

Does this need to be said by me? Even if something should be said, it might not be your responsibility. Someone else may be better positioned to speak.

Does this need to be said now? Timing matters. The best response at the wrong time can still fall short.

If the answer to any of those questions is no, don't respond. Wait. Let the moment breathe. See what happens. You might realize no response was needed at all.

The Fast Path from Reacting to Responding (or Not)

1. Notice when you feel compelled to respond.
Pay attention to the urge to reply, correct, or jump in. The first shift is simply recognizing the pattern.

2. Use the three-question filter before responding.
Does this need to be said? By me? Right now? Let those answers guide your choice.

3. Practice intentional silence in one situation.
Pick one area—meetings, email, family conversations—and challenge yourself to say less than you usually would.

4. Notice what happens when you do not respond.
Chances are, nothing bad will happen. The conversation will move on. Someone else may speak up. You will build confidence in your ability to pause.

The Awareness Path to Catching Your Response Impulse
This week, observe the moments when you feel pressure to respond. Ask yourself why. Is it to be heard? To be helpful? To control the outcome? You don't need to stop yourself every time. Just notice the impulse. That awareness alone creates space to choose differently next time.

Your What If Action

This week I will _____

_____

_____

_____

_____

_____

_____

_____

_____

_____

_____

_____

_____

_____

28.

WHAT IF THIS WEEK, YOU DID SOMETHING BECAUSE IT WAS HARD?

Being in recovery has shaped my life. Not just in living daily without a drink or drug but in how so many of the things I learned to stay clean and sober apply to everyday life. I wrote about it in my last book, *The Day Makes the Year (Makes a Life)*.

One of the bigger lessons was about doing hard things.

When I got into recovery, my life was a train wreck. I didn't want to quit drinking or drugging. I just wanted to get my father off my back. Since I had never actually tried to stop before, I had no idea what I was in for. It was hard. Way harder than I ever could have imagined.

Then one day this guy said to me, "Doug, this is the easier, softer way." That made no sense. How could something that felt so hard be the easier way?

It took time, but I learned he was right. Doing the hard thing—getting clean, staying clean, facing what I didn't want to face—turned out to be the path that made life better, easier. Not because it was easy, but because it worked.

That lesson didn't stay in recovery. It started showing up

everywhere. I realized that the hard thing I didn't want to do was usually the very thing that would create more peace, clarity, or confidence. Over time, I stopped avoiding hard just because it was hard. In fact, I started to seek it out.

Why Hard Things Matter

Most people associate hard things with stress, struggle, or survival. However, often, doing the hard thing is precisely what makes life easier in the long run.

You send the awkward text now so it doesn't become a bigger issue later. You say no to something small to protect your time for what matters most. You finish the project early. None of those are easy. But all simplify your day on the other side of the choice.

Doing something hard is how you create faster progress. It's how you reclaim clarity, calm, and confidence—one hard thing at a time. The hardest thing is often the fast track. It saves you hours of mental spinning, clears clutter from your calendar, and creates new momentum you've been waiting for. It reminds you of what you're capable of. Even one act of courage can elevate the way you see yourself.

The Beautiful Side of Difficult

Most people don't avoid hard things because they're lazy or fearful. They avoid them because they've practiced avoiding them. We're conditioned to default to comfort and convenience. That's not a flaw. It's human nature. But you can interrupt it.

The moment you notice a hard thing you could do, pause. Acknowledge the pull to skip it. Then ask what would change if you leaned in, just this once.

You'll be surprised how often doing the hard thing frees up your energy, clears your mental space, and makes the rest of your day feel lighter. The weight we carry is often the result of what we're avoiding.

That apology you've been meaning to make. That task you've procrastinated on for weeks. That limit you haven't enforced with someone who keeps overstepping. Those are not just friction points. They're invitations to lead your life instead of getting dragged through it.

Hard isn't always bad. Sometimes it's the beginning of better.

The Fast Path to Embracing Difficulty

1. Look for something that feels hard or uncomfortable this week.
A conversation you could have, a skill you could try, a boundary you could set. These aren't just pain points. They're potential launch points.

2. Ask what the benefits of doing it are.
Would it simplify your day? Build trust? Help you get noticed? Free up mental energy? Make someone else happy? Visualize the upside waiting for you.

3. Don't need to do it all at once.
Just start. A text. A sentence. A small action forward.

4. Let doing it shift how you see yourself.
Doing hard things on purpose builds proof. It shows you're choosing the stronger path, not just the easier one. Each time, you're building muscle and confidence.

The Awareness Path to Doing Hard on Purpose

This week, notice when you think, *That would be hard* or *I'll deal with that later.* Instead of seeing those moments as roadblocks, treat them as signals. What if that hard thing is a path to something better? You don't have to act on every hard thing. Just start viewing difficulty as a source of possibility, not something to avoid.

Your What If Action

This week I will _____

_____

_____

_____

_____

_____

_____

_____

29.

WHAT IF THIS WEEK, YOU LET YOUR ACTIONS COMMUNICATE YOUR GRATITUDE?

Most people think gratitude is a feeling. But what if it's a practice? Practicing gratitude shifts your focus from what's missing to what's present, from what's wrong to what's working. However, for most people, gratitude remains an internal experience—a thought, a feeling, or something they mention in passing.

My friend Steve once told me, "If you want to see my true gratitude, follow me around for the day." That line stuck with me. Until then, I thought of gratitude as a feeling. But he reminded me it's also a behavior.

Gratitude Is a Verb

Some of the happiest people I know are deeply grateful—not just for what they have but even for what they've overcome. More importantly, they carry that gratitude into how they show up in the world.

There's a saying in recovery: You can't keep what you don't give away. I think that's especially true when it comes to gratitude.

The Gratitude Spectrum

There are three types of gratitude.

Internal gratitude is the quiet appreciation you feel for something. It's when you pause to recognize what's good, what's steady, or what you've come through. It changes your perspective. But it's invisible to the people around you.

Reactive gratitude is the most common. It appears when something is offered to you: a kind gesture, a helpful word, or a thoughtful gift. You say thank you. You acknowledge what's been given. It matters.

Proactive gratitude takes it one step further. It doesn't wait. It creates opportunities. It's reaching out instead of responding. It's giving back before being asked. It's doing something kind because you remember what it felt like when someone did it for you.

The person who's quick to help because someone once helped them. The leader who mentors because someone once believed in them. The neighbor who checks in because they remember what it felt like to feel unseen. Their gratitude isn't just something they think. It's something they live.

Gratitude You Can See

When people try to deepen their sense of gratitude, they usually start by thinking more thankful thoughts. That matters. But the shift becomes real when it moves from internal to visible. The goal this week isn't to feel more thankful. It's to help someone else feel it too.

This could mean letting someone go ahead of you in traffic or at the grocery store. Complimenting someone's work in front of others. Tipping generously when service workers are doing their best. Leaving a handwritten thank-you note for someone who rarely gets recognition. Bringing someone their favorite coffee just because they've been showing up consistently.

These aren't grand gestures. They're simple acts that say "I notice" and "I appreciate." They turn internal gratitude into external impact.

The Fast Path to Gratitude in Action

1. Identify someone who has made a difference in your life.
Think of someone who supported, taught, or encouraged you in a way you'll never forget.

2. Find a way to demonstrate your gratitude through action this week.
Instead of merely saying thank you, show it by helping the person, honoring them, or passing their impact forward.

3. Look for one opportunity to be proactively grateful.
Don't wait for something nice to come your way. Create a moment for someone else.

4. Build one act of gratitude into your daily routine.
Choose something simple and repeatable. Send one thank-you message each day. Leave a positive comment. Take a moment to acknowledge someone's effort. When gratitude becomes part of your rhythm, it becomes part of your identity.

The Awareness Path to Moments of Appreciation

This week, take a moment to notice when you feel grateful and pause before moving on. Ask yourself, *What could I do right now to show this?* You might be surprised how often a small action is all it takes to make someone else feel seen and appreciated.

Your What If Action

This week I will _____

_____

_____

_____

_____

_____

_____

_____

_____

30.

WHAT IF THIS WEEK, YOU BEGAN LETTING GO OF A RESENTMENT?

I once heard someone talking about the hurt of not being invited to a college friend's wedding. What made it worse was discovering that others from their group were invited. The exclusion felt intentional and personal.

Years later, she was still carrying that weight. Every group text felt loaded. Every get-together carried an undercurrent of *Why wasn't I good enough for her wedding?* She found herself pulling back from people she liked, creating distance to protect herself from being hurt again.

Finally, she talked it over with a friend who told her something that stuck: "A hurt from years ago is keeping you from enjoying today. Let go of the hurt or let go of your friends. But you can't keep both."

She chose to let it go. The resentment was keeping her trapped in that moment of being excluded. Some resentments you can let go of in a week. Others, you can at least begin the process of release.

Or maybe it's different for you. Your friend shared something you told them in confidence. Your former partner ended the relationship suddenly, leaving you confused and hurt. Your boss took credit for your work in front of the leadership team.

We carry these resentments like stones in our pocket. They weigh us down, but we've gotten so used to the weight that we forget we're carrying them.

Until something reminds us, and the anger flares up all over again.

The Mental Bandwidth Thief

When I work with people who are stuck in resentment, they all have one thing in common: They're wasting enormous amounts of energy on something they can't change. They've given the hurt space in their head, and it's taking up room that could be used for better things.

The resentment becomes a constant drain. They rehearse what they should have said, imagine scenarios where the other person finally understands how much they hurt them, and build elaborate cases for why they're right and the other person is wrong.

Meanwhile, that person has probably moved on and is living their life while you're stuck managing yours around what they did to you.

The Beginning of Letting Go

Releasing a resentment doesn't happen overnight, but it can start this week. It begins with recognizing the cost of carrying it and deciding to stop paying that price.

You don't have to forgive completely. You don't have to forget what happened. You just have to decide you're tired of letting it control your mental space and emotional energy.

Someone close to me once said I should pray for anyone I had a resentment against. I couldn't stand the thought of praying for that person. But it gave me the catalyst to let it go, so I wouldn't have to. That decision was huge for me.

Stopping New Resentments Before They Take Root

Preventing resentments is easier than releasing them. When someone hurts or disappoints you, you have about twenty-four to forty-eight hours before that hurt hardens into something you'll carry for months or years.

The key is to catch it early—when you first feel slighted, overlooked, or wronged—and make a conscious choice not to dwell on it. Ask yourself: *Is this worth carrying?* Most of the time, the answer is no.

I've also found that examining my role in what happened is essential. Not that I did something wrong but that I might have contributed to what created the resentment in the first place. Review and release. It might not be easy, but it's certainly a lot easier than carrying it forward.

The Fast Path to Starting the Release

1. Identify one resentment you're ready to let go.

Pick something specific. A person, a situation, a hurt you've been carrying. You don't have to feel good about what happened; just decide you're tired of carrying it around.

2. Get clear on what it's costing you.

How is this resentment affecting your relationships, your energy, your ability to focus on what matters? Getting clear on the price you're paying makes it easier to choose to stop paying it.

3. Tell someone you trust that you're ready to release this.

Share what you're letting go of and ask them to help you stay focused on moving forward rather than staying stuck. Their perspective can be invaluable in letting the resentment go.

4. Make the decision and remind yourself when it tries to return.

Letting go is a decision, but the hurt may try to drag you back. When you catch yourself rehearsing what happened, remind yourself: "I've decided to let this go." You may need to make that choice multiple times, but each time you do, you reinforce your decision to move forward rather than staying stuck.

The Awareness Path to Catching Resentment's Grip

This week, notice when resentment flares up. Pay attention to how it affects your mood, your interactions, and your ability to be present. When you catch yourself rehearsing old hurts, ask: *Is this serving me? What would it feel like to redirect this energy toward something that matters now?* Starting to release resentment isn't about being OK with what happened; it's about acknowledging the pain and moving forward. It's about reclaiming your mental space for better things.

Your What If Action

This week I will

PRACTICE RELENTLESS SIMPLICITY

A Change & Growth Inflection Chapter

I used to joke that I could spend an entire afternoon organizing my to-do list and still not do anything. The truth is, it wasn't a joke. I was excellent at making things more complicated than they needed to be. Not because I wanted to avoid action but because overcomplicating felt productive. It gave me a false sense of control.

For a while, I convinced myself that what I needed was a better tool. I tried just about every productivity app or software you can think of. At one point, I was downloading something new every month. Then one day, I asked one of the most successful people I know to show me his system. He pulled out a notepad. That was it. A legal pad with a few handwritten priorities for the day. It was clear, low friction, and incredibly effective. That moment shifted my perspective on productivity and change.

Complexity doesn't create progress. It delays it.

Today, I still use a digital productivity tool—but only one. It's simple, has no bells or whistles, and I stick with it. That's the key. I stopped chasing systems and started trusting simplicity.

Over time, I've learned that complexity is often a form of procrastination. We keep researching. We keep tweaking. We keep refining plans. But deep down, we're usually avoiding the discomfort of starting. Of committing. Of doing the thing that moves us forward.

That's why I believe in practicing relentless simplicity.

It's not about dumbing things down or cutting corners. It's about cutting through noise and shrinking the decision. Stop asking twenty-seven questions and pick one that matters. That's why the What If Rule works. It simplifies the start.

If you find yourself overthinking, overplanning, or overcomplicating things, pause and ask:

What's the simplest next step I could take right now?

You don't need a perfect strategy. You don't need to know everything in advance. You just need a clear, uncomplicated move you can make today.

Simplicity gets you started.

Simplicity keeps you going.

Simplicity makes success repeatable.

Change and growth are challenging enough.

Don't overcomplicate them.

Practice relentless simplicity.

31.

WHAT IF THIS WEEK, YOU DID SOMETHING YOU'VE BEEN THINKING ABOUT THAT BRINGS YOU JOY?

Vera Wang didn't design her first wedding dress until she was forty. Up until then, she had been a competitive figure skater, a journalist, and a fashion editor. She wasn't trying to build a brand. She just wanted to create something for herself. Something that felt meaningful. Something that sparked joy.

That small decision became the beginning of one of the most iconic fashion careers in the world.

You don't have to start a business or reinvent your life. But what if this week, you took one step toward something that lights you up? The thing you've mentioned more than once. The idea you keep circling back to. The simple joy you've put off for later.

Joy Isn't Frivolous. It's Fuel.

We're really good at talking ourselves out of joy.

We say we don't have time, but we make time for everything else. We say we can't justify the money, but we spend on things that matter far less. We hesitate to call it important, because it's just something we'd enjoy.

I had a coaching client who became a good friend. Every few weeks, we'd meet for coffee and talk about life and work. One day, he mentioned he had always wanted to play guitar. I nodded, then realized he had said that exact thing at least three times over the past year.

So I asked him, "What if you just started this week?" He looked surprised, like the thought had never occurred to him. But he did it. He bought a used guitar that weekend and started with online tutorials.

Within a month, something shifted. Not just his ability to play a few chords but his entire energy. He'd come to our coffee meetings more relaxed, more animated. He started talking about other things he wanted to try. The guitar gave him permission to be a beginner again, to do something purely for the joy of it. It reminded him he was more than his job title.

That's the trap. We're taught that joy is optional. That responsible people don't prioritize joy—they earn it. But joy changes how you show up. It makes you more present, more creative, more grounded when things go sideways.

Bring On the Joy

When looking to do something just for joy, most people convince themselves it can wait. Everything else feels more urgent, more important, more justifiable. Joy gets pushed to "someday" like a reward we haven't quite earned yet.

But here's what happens when we keep postponing it: We start to forget what lights us up. We drift further from the things that make us feel alive. We become efficient at everything except being ourselves.

What brings you joy isn't just a luxury. It's a signal. It reminds you that you're more than what you produce or accomplish. When you act on that signal—even in a small way—it creates energy that ripples through everything else. You show up differently. You bring more life to your work, your relationships, your day.

The Fast Path from Thinking About Joy to Living It

1. Name what you've been thinking about.
What's the first thing that comes to mind when you read this question? What have you brought up more than once but never acted on? That's your starting point. Write it down.

2. Identify the real obstacle.
Is it time, money, or logistics? Or is it something deeper, like guilt, fear of being bad at it, or feeling like you don't deserve it? Be honest about what's really stopping you.

3. Start smaller if needed.
If the full version feels too big, scale it back. Want to take a painting class? Buy a few supplies and try it at home first. Want to learn piano? Download an app and try one lesson.

4. Do it imperfectly.
You don't have to be good. You don't have to finish. You don't have to share it with anyone. You just have to start.

The Awareness Path to More Joy

Notice what joyful thought you keep pushing aside. Pay attention to how quickly you dismiss it and what you say to yourself when you do. This week, try letting that idea stay on the table. Imagine what might shift if you gave it space.

Your What If Action

This week I will _____

_____

_____

_____

_____

_____

_____

_____

_____

_____

32.

WHAT IF THIS WEEK, YOU CHANGED ONE THING AT WORK OR HOME THAT NO LONGER SERVES YOU WELL?

Sometimes you get promoted but continue leading as if you're still in your old role. Sometimes the kids grow up but you're still treating them like they're seven. You've grown, but your habits haven't.

Or maybe it's subtler. You're frustrated, but you can't quite put your finger on the reason. Things feel heavier than they should. You're still doing what once made you successful, but it's no longer effective.

You're not failing. You've just outgrown your old approach.

Let It Go (Cue Elsa Singing)

I used to take pride in being fast, hands on, and direct. As a frontline manager, that style got results. The team respected me. The store performed. That version of me worked.

But as I stepped into higher leadership, it backfired. I needed to slow down, bring people with me, and develop other leaders. My strength—pushing through—had become a ceiling.

I didn't need to become someone else. I needed to utilize my strengths differently.

I know a parent who ran her household like a military operation when her kids were young. Schedules, chores, bedtimes—all managed with precision. It worked beautifully. The house ran smoothly, and everyone knew what to expect.

But as her children became teenagers, that same approach created constant conflict. They needed more autonomy, not more structure. Her ability to stay organized and in control had become a source of tension.

She didn't stop being the organizer. Instead, she shifted from managing their decisions to helping them make good ones. She kept the family calendar but allowed them to set their study schedules. She maintained household rules but involved them in creating consequences. It was the same strength, applied differently.

That's what happens when we overuse a strength—or fail to update it. We get attached to the behaviors that brought us success. They become part of our identity. I'm the one who gets it done. I'm the one who speaks up. I'm the one who holds it all together.

But what works in one phase of your life or career won't automatically work in the next.

When Familiar Becomes a Limitation

It's common to keep doing what used to work, even after it stops delivering the same results. Familiar habits feel efficient. Familiar roles feel safe. However, many people don't realize they've outgrown a behavior until it begins to create tension, confusion, or exhaustion.

It doesn't mean the behavior was wrong. It just means the

context has changed. Growth often means evolving your default—not replacing it but rather updating it to match who you are now and what this season requires. The question isn't whether something still feels familiar. It's whether it's still serving you. That's where the shift begins.

Remember this: The behaviors that got you here won't necessarily get you there.

The Fast Path from Outgrown to Evolved

1. Notice what you might be doing automatically that isn't working like it did.

What behaviors or responses have become so natural you don't think about them anymore, but they are creating friction or frustration?

2. Spot where it's creating friction.

Where do you feel stuck, tense, or ineffective? What feedback are you hearing and what are you ignoring? Where are you forcing something that used to feel natural?

3. Ask what this season actually needs.

Don't ask, "How do I fix this using what I know?" Instead ask, "What does this moment require from me now?"

4. Make one slight shift.

You don't have to change everything. Just choose one behavior or habit to approach differently this week.

The Awareness Path to Recognizing When You've Outgrown Your Approach

Pay attention this week to what you're doing on autopilot. Ask yourself if it still fits. When you let go of something that no longer serves you, you free up energy. You create space for what could work better. You might even see new possibilities you couldn't access using your old approach.

Your What If Action

This week I will

33.

WHAT IF THIS WEEK, YOU DIDN'T REACT TO SOMETHING OR SOMEONE THAT REGULARLY GETS UNDER YOUR SKIN?

You probably already know what triggers you. The coworker who talks over you. The driver who cuts you off. The neighbor's dog that won't stop barking. The one person who can change your mood with a single comment or glance. They do their thing, and you react. Every time. It feels automatic. But it doesn't have to be.

Your brain thinks it's helping. When something triggers you, it sends that signal straight to your emotional center before your logical brain can weigh in. That's why your jaw clenches. Why your heart rate spikes. Why something small feels like a personal offense.

This response made sense when we faced real danger. But today? It's just your neighbor's barking dog—or your coworker's tone.

Maybe you snap back. Maybe you stew silently. Perhaps you carry it with you longer than you care to admit. And nothing changes. Except now you feel worse.

But what if this week, you broke that pattern?

The Daily Annoyance Club

Most people think not reacting means stuffing it down and gritting your teeth. Pretending it doesn't bother you.

But that's not sustainable. And it's not what works.

I have a friend whose husband never closed the kitchen cupboards. It drove her crazy. Every open door felt like a message: He doesn't care about the things that matter to me.

She tried to ignore it. She told herself it wasn't a big deal. But it still irritated her. It felt forced. It didn't stick.

Then she tried something different. Every time she noticed an open cupboard, she would close it and immediately think of something kind her husband had done for her recently.

The irritation became a moment of gratitude. The trigger became a reminder of why she loved him. That wasn't suppression. That was retraining.

The Response Upgrade

When you stop reacting to every trigger, you stop handing over control of your mood to other people. You stay grounded instead of being pushed around by someone else's habits or tone.

You also defuse a lot of potential conflict. Most tension escalates because two people continue to react to each other. When you don't engage, there's nothing for the other person to push against.

It's easy to assume that certain people or situations just push your buttons. But reactivity isn't automatic. It's practiced.

Most people reinforce the pattern by replaying the frustration, venting about it later, or preparing for the next time. That keeps the trigger alive.

Real change begins by recognizing that the reaction is optional. It's yours to own. You may still feel the surge, but you can train yourself to resist feeding it. You can shift how you interpret it, how long it lasts, and what you choose to do next.

You can still care. You can still act. But you don't have to hand over your day to someone else's behavior.

The Fast Path from Reactive to Responsive

1. Identify your specific trigger.
Who or what consistently gets under your skin? Name it. Be specific about what they do that sets you off.

2. Plan your new response.
What will you do instead of reacting? Take a breath? Think of something you're grateful for? Redirect your attention? Choose ahead of time.

3. Practice the pause.
Create space between the moment something happens and what you do next. Even two or three seconds is enough to make a different choice.

4. Reframe the experience.
Can you look at the situation from a different perspective? Maybe the interrupting colleague is just excited. Perhaps the

barking dog belongs to someone who lives alone. A slight shift in perspective can change everything.

The Awareness Path to Noticing Your Triggers

Notice when your usual trigger shows up this week. Pay attention to how quickly your body tenses or your mind reacts. Even if you don't respond differently yet, the simple act of noticing is where change begins. You can't change what you don't see coming.

Your What If Action

This week I will _____

_____

_____

_____

_____

_____

_____

_____

_____

34.

WHAT IF THIS WEEK, YOU TOLD SOMEONE HOW MUCH THEY MEAN TO YOU?

I was in my home office, working like any other day, when my phone rang. I glanced at the caller ID and saw a name I hadn't seen in over fifteen years. It was a gentleman I had once terminated. To say I was surprised would be an understatement. Part of me hoped he wasn't calling to say he was parked in my driveway.

I answered with a cautious "Hello?" and he greeted me like it had only been a few months. I asked how he was doing. He said, "Not so good."

Then he said something that stopped me cold.

He was calling to thank me for firing him.

He told me how many chances I had given him, how he hadn't taken them. And how, even though it was painful at the time, getting fired had changed his life.

I had let him go for how poorly he treated his employees. He told me that moment had been a wake-up call because it made him realize he wasn't just treating his staff that way. He was treating his family that way too.

Then he said, "Doug, I have a terminal illness. I wanted to thank you because, without what you did, I wouldn't have had the kind of relationship I ended up having with my wife and two children. Thank you."

I didn't know what to say. My eyes filled with tears. I tried to respond, but all I could do was listen.

We spoke for a few more minutes. Then he said he had to go. I wished him peace with whatever he was facing. And I thanked him for the call.

That conversation changed my life in so many ways. Not because of what I had done. But because he took the time to say what most people don't.

When Thank You Goes Unsaid

It's not that we plan to send the message and never do. It's that we so often don't think to send it at all.

The teacher who believed in us when no one else did. The boss who took a chance on us. The coach who saw potential we couldn't see. The neighbor who showed up during our hardest moments. The friend who said exactly what we needed to hear.

They shaped us. Then life moved forward, and we never looked back to say thank you.

Not because we don't care. Because we haven't paused long enough to turn gratitude into action.

This week is your chance. You don't need to write a long message or reconnect for hours. You just need to let someone know they made a difference.

"I've never forgotten how you treated me." "Something you said stuck with me all these years." "You probably don't realize the impact you had on me."

That's it. Just real words, shared now while they can still be received.

The Fast Path to Expressing Gratitude

1. Choose someone who comes to mind right away.
Who do you think back to fondly because of the impact they had on you?

2. Keep it brief but say it out loud.
It doesn't have to be perfect. It just has to be personal. Even a single sentence can land deeply.

3. Don't wait for the perfect moment.
Perfect is the enemy of meaningful. Send that email or text when you have a moment. Or even better, call them.

4. Notice how it changes both of you.
Watch how their energy shifts. And notice what it does for you. Gratitude shared is rarely forgotten.

The Awareness Path to Unspoken Appreciation
Look around your life this week. Who has shaped you, supported you, or stood by you without ever being fully told how much it mattered? Notice when you think of someone with gratitude but don't act on it. What if this is the week you change that? What if those simple words will mean more to them than you'll ever know?

Your What If Action

This week I will _____

_____

_____

_____

_____

_____

_____

_____

_____

_____

_____

_____

_____

_____

LET GO OF THE MISS

A Change & Growth Inflection Chapter

I don't usually use sports analogies. They're often overdone, and they rarely fit how real people experience growth in everyday life.

But there's one I can't ignore.

Baseball.

Even the best hitters in the world miss more than they succeed. A .300 batting average is considered excellent. That means they fail to get a hit seven out of every ten times they step up to the plate.

But here's the part that matters: When they swing and miss—or strike out entirely—they don't carry that failure into the next at-bat. They don't walk up thinking about the last miss. They refocus. Reset. Step in like the next hit is about to come.

That mindset is everything.

Because the more you think you've failed, the harder it is to change and grow. Not because you actually can't but because your belief starts closing off the very actions that would help you move forward.

You get cautious. You hesitate. You play smaller. You stop trusting yourself.

Failure happens. But identifying with it—that's where people get stuck. One missed attempt turns into a story. That story turns into a pattern. And pretty soon, every new swing feels like a chance to confirm that you're not who you hoped you were.

That's the trap.

Remember, no one succeeds without missing. Growth demands mistakes, false starts, awkward phases, and doing things that don't work the first time.

The question is never "Did I fail?" The question is "Did I carry that miss into what comes next?"

You can't change the last swing. But you can change what you bring to the next one.

So let it go.

Let go of the miss. Let go of the story. Step up to the plate again—not because you're sure you'll get it right but because you're willing to keep swinging.

That's what separates the people who grow from the ones who stay stuck.

They don't overidentify with the last miss.

They just believe the next one will connect.

35.

WHAT IF THIS WEEK, YOU DID ONE THING THAT TAKES YOU OUTSIDE YOUR COMFORT ZONE?

Years ago, I hired a young woman who was great with customers. I knew she'd thrive in sales. She took a cashier position instead and would always say, "Oh no, I could never sell."

Until one day, she said she'd try. And she crushed it.

So I said, "You'd be a great manager." Again, she said no. Then one day—yes. She agreed to try an entry-level leadership role. She was excellent.

Every time she leveled up, she hesitated first. But each time, she eventually said yes.

A few years later, I watched her win an award for managers. That moment didn't happen all at once. It happened gradually, every time she chose to move past her comfort zone.

Let's talk about why that matters.

Your Comfort Zone Says It's Ready for a Change.

We say we stay in our comfort zone because it's smart. Responsible. Safe.

However, the truth is that comfort zones don't keep us safe. They keep us small.

That voice you're waiting for—the one that says, "You're ready"? It usually doesn't show up first. It shows up after. After the brave step. After the shaky yes. After the thing you thought you couldn't do.

The person with ideas worth sharing? They only show up when you speak.

The leader others want to follow? They only emerge when you step forward.

The real, creative, bold version of yourself? You meet them outside the pattern of what feels easy.

Every time you choose familiar over growth, you're choosing the version of you that exists over the one that's waiting.

When You Answer the Call

You discover that fear shrinks when you move toward it.

You access traits that comfort can't reach—courage, clarity, and boldness. They don't develop in neutral. They show up in motion.

You start seeing more. More opportunities. More capacity. More of what's possible.

You begin to trust yourself differently. Not because someone told you you're ready but because you proved it.

And you realize that the most significant risk isn't doing the thing that makes you uncomfortable. It's getting stuck in a version of yourself that stopped growing.

The Uncertain Feeling of Growth

Most people wait for confidence before they take a leap. But waiting can become a habit. Growth typically emerges amid uncertainty, not after it has been resolved. The hesitation you feel doesn't mean you're not ready. It means you're entering new territory.

Progress begins when you're willing to feel unsure and move anyway. Even one small stretch can open the door to new insight, strength, and trust in yourself. The version of you who can do the thing is shaped by doing it. Not all at once. Just one action that breaks the pattern of staying where it's safe. That's how you begin to expand what's possible.

The Fast Path Beyond Your Comfort Zone

1. Identify what feels slightly uncomfortable.
Not overwhelming. Just a stretch. The thing you've been holding back. The conversation you've avoided. The move you've been quietly considering.

2. Choose courage over comfort.
Remind yourself that the next version of you isn't inside your comfort zone. It's waiting just past it.

3. Start before you feel ready.
Confidence doesn't come first. Action does. Go before you feel brave—and let bravery catch up.

4. Focus on growth, not outcome.
Whether it works or doesn't isn't the point. The win is doing the thing you usually wouldn't.

The Awareness Path to Growth Moments

This week, catch yourself in those moments when you're about to choose the safe option. When you feel that little tug toward staying small. That discomfort you're trying to avoid? It's not a stop sign. It's a compass pointing toward the person you're becoming.

Your What If Action

This week I will _____

_____

_____

_____

_____

_____

_____

_____

_____

36.

WHAT IF THIS WEEK, YOU DIDN'T TAKE SOMETHING PERSONALLY?

I've published a weekly newsletter for years. Any time someone unsubscribed, I took it personally. I mean, I put real thought into this newsletter. Why wouldn't they want to keep reading?

One day, a woman who had been on the list for years unsubscribed. I noticed her name because she had replied to past editions, shared encouragement, and even forwarded it to others. Why would she unsubscribe?

So I did something I probably shouldn't have. I emailed her.

I was polite. I just said I noticed she unsubscribed and was curious if she'd share why. Was it something I said? Something I could do better?

A couple of days later, I got a reply. But not from her. It was from her daughter.

She let me know that her mother had passed away. She told me how much her mom had loved the newsletter, how she looked forward to it each week, and how she often shared it with friends. They were simply closing out her accounts.

I have never felt so small.

Not because I was embarrassed, though I was. I realized how

quickly I had made that moment about me. Her absence. Her silence. Her departure from my list. I assumed it was a statement. A judgment. A rejection. But it wasn't any of those things.

That's the trap. We confuse approval with validation. When we don't get it, we make it about our worth.

It reminds me of one of my favorite movie lines. In *Beaches*, Bette Midler's character looks across the table and says, "But enough about me. Let's talk about you. What do you think of me?"

It's funny because it's true.

The Validation Trap

We all want to be seen, liked, and understood. There's nothing wrong with that. But when we start needing it—when we hand over our emotional state to someone else's response—we give away our stability.

That short reply? That silence? That unfollow or skipped invite? It might not mean what you think it means. It might not mean anything at all.

But if you take it personally, it becomes a wound rather than a moment.

This week's What If isn't about shutting down emotionally. It's about not outsourcing your worth to someone else's reaction.

The Fast Path to Reclaiming Your Self-Worth

1. Notice the approval pull.
When something stings this week, ask yourself: *Am I looking for validation here?* Just naming it can loosen its grip.

2. Reframe your response.
A lack of praise isn't an insult. A delay isn't rejection. An unsubscribe isn't a statement about your value. People are busy. People are human.

3. Close the loop internally.
Before you look outward for reassurance, try offering it inward. *I put in the effort. I did good work. I'm proud of that.*

4. Let others have their response.
You don't have to manage or decode other people's reactions. Let them feel what they feel. You stay steady in who you are.

The Awareness Path to Standing Strong
At some point this week, something might feel personal. A reaction, a silence, a comment. When it happens, pause and ask, "Why am I making this about me?" Then ask, "What else might be true?" You can care deeply about people without handing them the keys to your self-worth.

Your What If Action

This week I will _____

37.

WHAT IF THIS WEEK, YOU CAUGHT YOURSELF ADDING DIALOGUE TO CONVERSATIONS?

A friend mentions they're running late to meet you. Before they finish explaining about traffic, you might decide they don't respect your time. But they just got stuck in traffic.

You share an idea in a meeting, and a colleague raises a concern. It's easy to assume they think your idea is stupid. Or that you are. But they're just wondering how it would work.

You text someone, and they don't respond. Within hours, you could write an entire story about why they're ignoring you, what you did wrong, or how they must be annoyed. But they just got busy.

This phenomenon occurs so frequently that psychologists have given it a name. Mind reading is when you assume you know what someone else is thinking without evidence. Cognitive distortions occur when your brain distorts reality, making what's happening seem more dramatic, negative, or personal than it is. These patterns usually come from past experiences, but once you notice them, you can respond differently.

The Voice-Over in Your Head

Adding dialogue means hearing what was never said. Someone speaks, and you fill in the blanks with your fears, history, and assumptions.

Most of what we insert isn't about the person in front of us. It's about the past. The teacher who made you feel foolish. The parent who always had a correction. The boss who never approved. The culture that trained you to stay quiet.

These old messages don't just play in the background. They rewrite the conversation.

You start hearing judgment where there was only feedback. Distance where there was just distraction. Criticism where there was only curiosity.

When the Story Gets in the Way

I was leading a program for frontline managers. Throughout the day, participants provided feedback to one another during role-playing exercises. I noticed one woman shut down every time someone spoke to her. Even the most thoughtful suggestions landed like criticism.

At lunch, I pulled her aside and said, "I can see you bracing before anyone even finishes their sentence."

She nodded. "I just always assume I've messed something up."

So I gave her one challenge for the afternoon: Listen to the exact words. No interpreting. No analyzing. Just take in what's being said and respond to that, not the meaning you assign to it.

The shift was noticeable. She became more open. More engaged. More relaxed. The stories she'd been telling herself weren't just exhausting—they were getting in the way.

I don't know where those old messages came from, but I know they were keeping her stuck. And maybe the same is true for you.

The First Shift Is Awareness

The goal isn't to stop reacting. It's to start noticing. Most people don't realize when they're adding meaning because the story arrives faster than the facts. Your brain fills in gaps automatically, usually based on past experiences rather than current reality.

When you feel a reaction rising, pause and try to identify the old tape that's playing. That moment of curiosity breaks the loop. You don't have to silence every thought. You just need to create enough space to question whether the thought is true.

The Fast Path to Hearing What's Really Said

1. Notice when you're reacting to your interpretation.

Pay attention to when your response is based on what you think they meant rather than what they said.

2. Ask yourself: What did they actually say?

Get literal. "I don't think that idea will work" is feedback on the idea, not your intelligence. "I see it differently" is not "You're wrong."

3. Respond to their words, not your story.

If someone questions a detail, answer the question. If they offer a different view, engage with their point, not the imagined judgment behind it.

4. *Check your assumptions.*

If you're unsure what someone meant, ask. "When you said X, did you mean Y?" Most misunderstandings evaporate with a straightforward question.

The Awareness Path to Catching Your Interpretations

Notice this week when your reaction is based on tone, timing, or assumption rather than actual words. Pay attention to how quickly you jump from what someone says to what you think they mean. Most of the time, the gap between those two things is where the misunderstanding lives. When you stop writing both sides of the conversation, the real one becomes a lot easier to hear.

Your What If Action

This week I will

38.

WHAT IF THIS WEEK, YOU DID SOMETHING SPECIAL FOR SOMEONE WHO COULD USE A BOOST?

I was working late at Bose on a big project that was due the next morning. The office was emptying, and I was feeling the pressure of the deadline when a colleague stopped by my desk on his way out.

"Have a good night," he said, already coat in hand, clearly ready to head home.

"Once I get this project done," I replied, not looking up from my screen.

Without hesitation, he took his coat off and set it down.

"What can I help with?" he asked.

He didn't have to do that. He had his evening plans. But he saw someone who could use support, and he chose to offer it.

I've never forgotten that moment. Not just because his help got me out of there earlier but because of what it felt like to have someone notice I was struggling—and do something about it.

The Oscar-Worthy Performance of "I'm Fine"

Most people are walking around carrying more than they show. The colleague who seems fine might be dealing with a sick parent. The friend who's been quieter than usual might be struggling at home. The family member who's always showing up for others might be running on empty themselves.

We often become so focused on our challenges that we overlook opportunities to make a difference in someone else's day. We notice when someone seems upset, but we miss the quieter signs—fatigue, withdrawal, stress—that someone could use a lift.

The most meaningful gestures often come from noticing what's not being said.

The Ninja Move of Caring

Once you start looking, you'll see opportunities everywhere.

The real opportunity isn't in reacting to obvious struggles. It's in noticing what most people miss. You're not looking for someone in crisis. You're looking for someone carrying more than they're saying. Someone who's steady on the outside but stretched thin underneath.

That's where a well-timed gesture hits the deepest—when it's unexpected, when it shows that someone is paying attention. When it says, "I see you."

Then take action that's specific and personal. Not generic encouragement—real support. Not "Let me know if I can help"—actual help.

Drop off their favorite coffee. Send a message that conveys what you appreciate about them. Offer to take something off their plate. Make them laugh when they need it most. Get them food from their favorite restaurant.

Small, well-timed gestures stick. They create a ripple. They shift your mindset from inward pressure to outward purpose. And they often land at just the right moment—even if you never know it.

The person you lift might turn around and lift someone else. They might even see themselves differently because of what you saw in them.

The Fast Path to Boosting Someone's Day

1. Pick someone specific who could use a boost.
Think about who's been carrying a lot lately. Who seems a little off? Who's been unusually quiet?

2. Do something personal and thoughtful.
Make it specific to them and what they'd appreciate. Personal beats generic every time.

3. Do it when they least expect it.
The surprise multiplies the impact. A random gesture on a regular day beats a routine gesture on a birthday.

4. Enjoy the good feeling that comes from giving.
This is "Give to Get" in action. You're not doing it for recognition. You're doing it for the quiet joy of knowing you made someone's day better.

The Awareness Path to Seeing Who Needs a Boost
This week, pay attention to who might be carrying more

than they're showing. Who seems a little off? Who's been unusually quiet? Who do you keep meaning to check in on but haven't yet? You don't have to fix anything. Just start noticing. Awareness is the first step toward meaningful action.

Your What If Action

This week I will

_____

_____

_____

_____

_____

_____

_____

_____

_____

39.

WHAT IF THIS WEEK, YOU CALMLY AND CLEARLY RESPONDED WHEN SOMEONE DISRESPECTED YOU?

Most people handle disrespect in one of three ways: ignoring it, carrying it, or overreacting.

They don't want to seem difficult, so they let it slide. Or they dwell on it for days, replaying what they should have said. Eventually, they snap or stay silent. Neither helps.

Here's the thing: Most disrespect doesn't need to become a big deal. It just needs to be handled.

You have two simple choices.

You can let it go. Especially when the person's opinion doesn't matter or their behavior isn't worth your energy. I do this when I don't respect the person. It's not passive. It's intentional.

Or you can respond clearly and calmly. Not to punish. Not to prove a point. Just to move the moment forward in a different direction.

When People Forget Their Manners
A former colleague of mine worked on a leadership team where she was the only woman in the room. The men weren't openly

rude, but they interrupted her constantly. They rarely asked for her input. They talked over her during meetings.

At first, she brushed it off. Told herself it didn't matter, that they didn't mean anything by it.

But over time, it did matter. Not because she lacked confidence but because the pattern was real—and it was getting in the way of her doing her job.

So I suggested a simple shift. Just one calm, clear phrase she could use in the moment.

"Going forward, I'd appreciate the chance to finish before someone else speaks."

She didn't say it with frustration. She didn't say it to start a fight. She said it with steady, forward energy.

And it worked.

They didn't instantly become the most respectful team in the world. But they paused. They noticed. And the tone started to shift.

More importantly, she shifted. She stopped carrying the frustration and started working from a stronger place.

The Better Way

When people don't respond to disrespect, it's rarely because they're weak. It's because they don't see a clean way to handle it. They think their only options are to bottle it up or blow it up.

But there's a better way.

You can let it go. Fully. Without carrying it around. Or you can say one thing that moves things forward.

That's it. Not a fight. Not a lecture. Not a long explanation. Just one clean, clear moment.

The forward-focused response works because nobody can

get too defensive about something that hasn't happened yet. You're not calling someone out. You're calling attention to what comes next.

That's how you stop carrying the weight of someone else's behavior. And start taking ownership of your own.

The Fast Path to Handling It

1. Notice what kind of disrespect gets to you.
It might be being talked over, dismissed, teased, ignored, or excluded. Recognizing the pattern helps you catch it sooner.

2. Decide: Let it go or shift it forward.
If it doesn't impact your work or your well-being, release it. If it lingers or holds you back, it needs a response.

3. Use a forward phrase.
Try something like, "I'd appreciate being included in the next decisions" or "Let me finish my thought, then I'd love to hear yours" or "From now on, I'd prefer we handle it this way."

4. Stay calm and clear.
You don't need to escalate or justify. You just need to say it. That's the shift.

The Awareness Path to Not Carrying It
Notice what you carry after a conversation. If you feel tight, annoyed, or unsettled, take a moment to check in. Was it a matter of disrespect, or your silence in response to it? Either way, you still have the option to choose how to clear it.

Your What If Action

This week I will

WHAT YOU DON'T SEE CAN SLOW YOU DOWN

A Change & Growth Inflection Chapter

Most of us learned to drive without the luxury of blind spot warning systems. You had to check over your shoulder before changing lanes. You had to remember that your mirrors didn't show the whole picture.

I still remember the day I learned that lesson the hard way.

Early in my driving life, I got comfortable just using my mirrors. I thought I had it down. Until I didn't. I caused a minor accident that could have been worse. Lesson learned. Even now, with a car that lights up and beeps when someone's in my blind spot, I still turn and look.

That moment taught me something I've come back to again and again. Blind spots don't exist just on the road. They show up in how we listen, how we react, how we communicate, and how we see ourselves and the people around us.

The tricky part is that blind spots are often invisible until something or someone helps you see them.

They're not just things you overlook. They're things you don't even realize you're missing. And they can quietly slow down your growth without you ever noticing.

But once you spot one, you can start to spot more.

You start to understand why something keeps tripping you up.

Why a relationship feels off. Why a pattern keeps repeating. And more importantly, you gain the power to change it.

That's the hidden value of blind spots. Yes, they carry risk. But they also hold a reward. Growth doesn't come just from pushing forward. It comes from seeing what you haven't seen before.

Ask people you trust what you might be missing. Pay attention to the feedback that makes you bristle. Listen closely when something familiar keeps going wrong.

You don't need to be perfect. You just need to be open.

Because what you can't see can slow you down.

But once you're willing to see it, it can also set you free.

40.

WHAT IF THIS WEEK, YOU BECAME YOUR OWN BEST ADVOCATE?

Carol didn't resent anything she was doing. She just couldn't keep doing all of it.

Even before the pandemic, she was the one people leaned on. The one who made the schedules work. The one who kept the energy up, prepared the meals, answered the group texts, and helped the family move forward. During the pandemic, the load only grew. And she carried it without complaint. But she was running on fumes.

One afternoon, in the middle of folding laundry and answering texts from her family, a fleeting thought crossed her mind: *I need a weekend to recharge.*

The thought passed quickly, brushed aside by guilt, timing, and a dozen reasons why it wasn't possible. But it had surfaced for a reason.

Later that week, she remembered the line they say on every flight: "Put your oxygen mask on first." She'd heard it a hundred times. But this time, it landed differently.

She realized that advocating for herself wasn't selfish. It was necessary. Not so that she could keep going. So she could stop disappearing.

Speaking Up for Your Work

Most people don't struggle to care for others. They struggle to include themselves.

Whether it's a mom who never takes a break, a team player who always says yes, or someone who avoids speaking up because they don't want to seem difficult, the result is the same. You quietly vanish behind your responsibilities.

You start to believe that being strong means being silent. That good people don't ask for much. The need for something makes you less valuable.

You can love others deeply and still advocate for yourself. You can be generous and still have boundaries. You can carry a lot and still put something down.

Being your own best advocate doesn't mean you stop caring about others. It means you finally start including yourself in that care.

When Caring Includes You

I once worked with a woman who was awesome at her job. She was steady and incredibly dependable. She never missed a deadline. She kept things organized. People loved working with her. But she wasn't the loudest voice in the room, and over time, she saw other people who were more visible but not necessarily more capable getting the opportunities she hoped for.

At first, she was frustrated. Then she decided to do something about it. She told me, "I know I do good work. I'm also starting to see that people take me for granted." I reminded her that the only person who can change that is her.

She wasn't going to turn into someone who shouted, "Look at me." That wasn't her. But she *could* start naming what she wanted. Sharing what she was proud of. Speaking up when it mattered. Even if it was uncomfortable.

She didn't need to become someone different. She just needed to become someone who had her own back. And she did just that. She didn't move up in the company. She got an even better job with another company.

Advocacy Starts Small

We often imagine self-advocacy as a big moment. It must be a dramatic conversation, a bold request, or a public declaration. But most of the time, it's quieter than that.

It's saying, "Actually, that doesn't work for me."

It's asking, "Can I take a break?" before you're on the verge of burnout.

It's telling someone, "Here's something I did this week I'm proud of."

It's choosing to rest without guilt. It's speaking up in the small moments instead of waiting to be noticed. It's asking for what you need rather than hoping someone will guess.

These aren't grand gestures. They're quiet acts of self-respect. And that's where your voice becomes your best advocate.

The Fast Path to Self-Advocacy

1. Notice where you're feeling unrecognized or unsupported.
At home or work, where are you carrying too much without being acknowledged?

2. Say something you usually keep to yourself.
A need. An idea. A feeling. It doesn't have to be bold. Just true.

3. Take one action that prioritizes you.
Ask for the time. Say no to the extra task. Take the break. These aren't luxuries. They're signs of self-respect.

4. Celebrate one quiet win.
You don't need someone else to clap for it. You just need to see it. Advocacy starts with recognition. From you.

The Awareness Path to Your Silent Moments

This week, notice when you stay quiet about something that matters to you. Like when you don't mention what you need, avoid asking for what you want, or wait to be chosen instead of advocating for yourself. Pay attention to that moment when you think *I should speak up* but don't. Ask yourself: *What if I said something?* Being your own best advocate doesn't make you selfish—it makes you sustainable.

Your What If Action

This week I will

41.

WHAT IF THIS WEEK, YOU ACCEPTED SOMEONE FOR WHO THEY ARE?

One of my employees once came to me wanting to quit. She couldn't stand working with another team member. *Hate* might not even be a strong enough word for how she felt. The situation had become so unbearable that she was ready to walk away from a job she loved and a company she valued, all because of one difficult relationship.

Before accepting her resignation, I asked her to try something different. I challenged her to try accepting this colleague for who they were, not for their sake but for her own.

What worked was realizing she didn't have to like the person. She didn't have to excuse their behavior or pretend it was OK. But by accepting them as they were—acknowledging that this was simply who they were and how they operated—she could move forward without absorbing the negativity.

She stayed. And she was glad she did. The other person never changed, but everything about the relationship did. Once she stopped trying to change them, she was able to deflect their behavior instead of taking it on.

The Exhausting Art of People Changing

We waste enormous energy trying to change people who have no interest in changing. We argue, reason, get frustrated, and burn ourselves out trying to make them see things differently or behave better.

I know a woman who struggled for years with her older sister. She felt her sister had been mean to her—critical, dismissive, always finding fault—since childhood. Every family gathering became a minefield of potential conflict.

When her sister passed away unexpectedly, that pain intensified. There was no longer any possibility of the relationship she'd always hoped for. All those years of trying to get her sister to be kinder, more supportive, more loving—none of it had worked.

Eventually, she turned inward. She began to accept her sister for who she had been—difficult, sometimes even cruel, but also someone carrying her own pain and limitations. She couldn't change what had happened, but she could change how she carried it. She found peace through that acceptance, though she wished she had done it while her sister was still alive.

When You Stop Fighting Reality

We're often told to accept people but rarely are shown how to do so. That's because acceptance is seldom a monumental moment. It's a quiet decision to stop resisting what's already there.

Acceptance doesn't mean tolerating unacceptable behavior. You can accept that a coworker is someone who takes credit for others' work while still protecting your contributions. You can accept that a relative makes inappropriate comments while still setting boundaries on what you'll tolerate.

Acceptance is not approval. It's freedom from the need to change what you can't control. When you stop hoping someone will suddenly become different, you stop being surprised by what they've always done. You become more grounded in reality. And from that place, your response becomes more intentional, more protective, and far less reactive.

The Fast Path to Accepting Reality

1. Pick one person who frustrates or disappoints you.
Think of someone you keep hoping will change but never does. Start with one relationship where you've been resisting reality.

2. Identify what you need to accept about them.
What behaviors or traits do you keep expecting to be different? Write down what you need to acknowledge as simply part of who they are.

3. Decide what you won't accept and how you'll respond.
Acceptance isn't approval. Define your boundaries and how you'll enforce them without trying to fix or change the person.

4. Focus on your side of the relationship.
What's within your control? What will change about the way you respond now that you're no longer trying to change them?

The Awareness Path to Your Change-Them Impulse
This week, pay attention to how often you try to change someone else. It may show up as disappointment, frustration, sarcasm, or subtle attempts to encourage them to act differently.

Every time you notice it, pause and ask yourself: *Am I trying to change them? Or can I accept who they are and choose a different response?* Remember: You are 100 percent responsible for 50 percent of every relationship.

Your What If Action

This week I will _____

_____

_____

_____

_____

_____

_____

_____

_____

_____

_____

_____

42.

WHAT IF THIS WEEK, YOU MOVED FORWARD WITHOUT HAVING IT ALL FIGURED OUT?

One of the most challenging consulting engagements I ever had was with a business owner whose company was barely hanging on. Sales were dropping. Morale was low. Bills were piling up.

When we discussed next steps, he would freeze. He had ideas. Lots of them. He'd lay out detailed possibilities and backup plans. But he wouldn't act. Not one new strategy. Not one call. Not one email. Not one change.

He wasn't lazy. He was overwhelmed and stuck in his head. Playing out every scenario, obsessing over every possible risk. He wasn't just overthinking. He was underdoing.

Finally, I told him, "Pick one thing. Do it this week. We'll figure out the rest as we go." He chose to call three former clients who hadn't ordered in months. Two of them placed orders that week—not because he used the perfect strategy but because it was a strategy he actually executed.

That's when I started to notice it everywhere. The more we think, the more we spin. And the more we spin, the less we move.

The Analysis Paralysis Club

Overthinking is one of the fastest ways to stall momentum. It often starts with good intentions: exploring different angles, considering risks, mentally rehearsing what's ahead. But before long, it becomes a loop—more scenarios, more analysis, less clarity.

While overthinking can appear to be preparation, it's often fear in disguise. Fear of failing. Fear of being wrong. Fear that the choice we make won't be the perfect one. So we pause. Wait. Circle the options one more time.

Here's what I've learned: Overthinking usually isn't about the future. It's often the past hijacking the present. That time you made the wrong call at work. That relationship decision you regret. That investment that didn't pan out. Those old experiences whisper, "You better think this through completely, or you'll mess up again."

But the fact is this: You can't think your way to certainty. You can only act your way to clarity.

Feet First, Head Second

Progress doesn't happen in your head. It happens in your day.

You can only take action from where you are. Not from where you wish you were. Not from where you were before. Right here. Right now.

That's why one of the most powerful tools to use when you start spinning is this: Keep your thoughts where your feet are. It's about focusing on what's actually in front of you rather than all the scenarios in your head.

What's happening now? What step can I take here? What does moving forward look like in this moment?

START WITH *WHAT IF*

I knew a couple who spent so much time trying to figure out what color and type of paint to use on their house that it took them years, while the house slowly deteriorated. They researched paint types, consulted color wheels, bought sample after sample, and debated finishes endlessly. Meanwhile, the old paint was peeling, and the wood was starting to rot.

Finally, their neighbor said, "Just pick five colors and paint them on a section on the back of the house." They did, then the couple invited the neighbors and a few more people over to see the samples. Everyone ultimately agreed on a single color. The couple had the house painted within a month. It looked great, and they wondered why they'd waited so long. Sometimes the cost of not deciding is higher than making the "wrong" decision.

If you need to break free from overthinking, the secret isn't more thinking. Its movement. It's taking a small action rooted in the present. That's how you shift momentum. That's how you grow.

The Fast Path to Moving Forward Anyway

1. Catch yourself in the overthinking loop.
Notice when your thinking turns from planning into spinning. If you're revisiting the same thoughts without action, you're probably overthinking.

2. Name the fear underneath it.
Is it fear of getting it wrong? Looking like you don't know what to do? Losing control? You don't have to fix the fear. Just call it out. Naming it reduces its grip.

3. Get your thoughts to where your feet are.
Bring your focus back to where you are. Ask yourself: *What's one simple thing I can do right here, right now?*

4. Celebrate forward movement.
Even the tiniest action matters. Overthinkers tend to overlook small wins. Don't. A small win is a start. It's the end of the loop and the beginning of traction.

The Awareness Path to Present-Moment Action
This week, when you feel stuck in analysis or overwhelmed by options, pause and look down at your feet. That's where you are. That's where your next action lives. You don't need the whole plan figured out to take one step. Notice how much clearer things become when you focus on what's actually in front of you instead of all the scenarios in your head.

Your What If Action

This week I will _____

_____

_____

_____

_____

_____

43.

WHAT IF THIS WEEK, YOU GIVE YOUR MIND SOME EXTRA SPACE EACH DAY?

Some readers may find this What If easy. Others will find it surprisingly hard. I used to be one of the latter.

Once my day started, it didn't stop. I moved quickly, spoke quickly, and worked quickly. I thought momentum meant progress. But what it meant was that I rarely gave my mind a moment to breathe.

I remember being in a meeting one afternoon and looking out the window. A few employees were walking the loop outside, chatting casually as they passed by. I used to call them "corporate walkers." It seemed like a luxury I couldn't afford. Who has time for that?

Turns out, I did. I just didn't realize yet how much I needed it.

Over time, I learned that constant motion doesn't equal clarity. Some of my best thinking, calmest moments, and most centered decisions now happen when I give myself a little space—mentally and physically. A short walk. A few still minutes between meetings. Sitting outside before heading home. That space doesn't slow me down. It resets me. And it makes me sharper.

When Your Brain Won't Shut Up

Your brain isn't built to run nonstop. When you give it no space, it gets loud, cluttered, and reactive. When you provide it with space, it clears. It settles. It breathes.

Mental space helps you shift from noise to presence, from reaction to a more considered perspective. It's not about doing nothing. It's about giving yourself room to think, process, and just be.

It's like the words in this book. Sentences need space. So do paragraphs. Without it, the whole thing would be one giant run-on. And it wouldn't work for you, the reader, or for me, the writer.

Playing Hide-and-Seek with Free Time

It starts with deciding to find and use the space. It's there. No matter how busy you are, you have the space. I'm positive you do. You may not have seen it before, most likely because you haven't been looking for it.

It's like when you start thinking about buying a new car. Suddenly, you're seeing all these different cars around you that you overlooked before. The space was always there.

Remember, you're just seeking some extra space. You don't need to find an hour in your day, unless you've decided that's what you want. A few minutes in the car before walking into the office. Sitting outside for fifteen minutes before the kids arrive home. A short walk without your phone. A pause at the park between errands.

It's not wasted time. It's recovery. It's clarity. It's you showing up better for what and who matters next.

The Fast Path to Mental Breathing Room

1. Identify when your mind could use a break.
Perhaps it's during your commute, between meetings, while preparing dinner, or after certain conversations. Look for a moment where your mind tends to stay active but doesn't need to be.

2. Choose one pocket of time to create it.
This could be five minutes before walking into the office, after school drop-off, during a quiet lunch, or while on a short walk at the end of the day. Don't overthink it. Find a moment to protect.

3. Remove input. Add stillness.
No email. No scrolling. No "catching up." This isn't a break to get things done. It's a break to let things go.

4. Pay attention to what emerges.
Notice how you feel afterward. What surfaces when the noise settles? Ideas. Clarity. Calm. You don't have to chase answers. Sometimes they show up when you stop running.

The Awareness Path to Finding Mental Space
Start by noticing when your mind feels full. Most of us are so accustomed to being overstimulated that we no longer even realize it. You refresh your inbox out of habit. You scroll between meetings. You fill silence with noise. This week, catch yourself in those moments. Ask the space question: "What if I just sat with this quiet instead of filling it?" Experience

the sensation of leaving a little space instead of immediately reaching for more input.

Your What If Action

This week I will _____

_____

_____

_____

_____

_____

_____

_____

_____

_____

_____

_____

WHAT YOU DO IS WHO YOU BECOME

A Change & Growth Inflection Chapter

There was a period in my life when I felt like everything had gotten boring. My days felt flat. Nothing excited me. I remember telling a friend how dull everything had become. I was expecting empathy.

Instead, he laughed and said, "Maybe it's because you're boring."

It hit me sideways. I was a little stunned, maybe even insulted. I had come to him looking for understanding, not a punchline. But like many things that hit a nerve, I couldn't stop thinking about it. I ran it through my head over and over. And eventually, something started to shift.

What was he really saying to me?

Not that I was a boring person by nature. But I was showing up in a way that created boredom. I wasn't doing much. I wasn't curious. I wasn't putting energy into anything new. I had fallen into a pattern where every day looked the same, and I expected the excitement to just show up.

It's easy for that to happen. Especially as you get older. You take on responsibilities. You have a career. Maybe kids. Your identity shifts without you even noticing. And if you're not careful, you lose yourself in the routine. You stop doing the things that fuel you. And without that fuel, change and growth slow down.

That moment forced me to take a hard look at how I was living. And the truth was hard to ignore.

I wasn't bored.

I was being boring.

And the only way to change that was to start doing things that lit me up. Not all at once. Not in a dramatic way. But with small, deliberate decisions. Try something different. Say yes when I usually say no. Add a little adventure to an ordinary day.

Because your identity isn't something you find—it's something you create. You are what you do. And growth depends on doing. When you stop engaging, you stop evolving.

Just remember: What you do is who you become.

44.

WHAT IF THIS WEEK, YOU RETURNED TO A COMMITMENT YOU MADE TO YOURSELF?

Returning to a commitment you made to yourself might sound simple. Maybe too simple. But almost everyone struggles with it.

You say you won't eat ice cream on weekdays. You'll stop scrolling after 10 p.m. You'll tackle that project you've been avoiding. And then life happens. Or stress happens. Or boredom or pressure or just that little voice that says, "You've already messed it up, so why not?" (I use that one on the way to the freezer.)

There's no shame in it. But it can erode your confidence more than you realize. Every time you break a commitment to yourself, it chips away at your belief that next time will be different. Eventually, your word to yourself stops holding weight.

Not because you're weak but because your brain is wired for comfort, not consistency, and when comfort is close and consistency is hard, your brain will talk you out of the hard thing.

But here's the flip side. Just one kept commitment—especially when it's small and specific—can start rebuilding your trust in yourself. It creates a mini proof point. One notch in the belt of self-belief. And that's often all you need to start shifting the pattern.

It doesn't have to be dramatic. It could be as small as clearing the kitchen counter each night before bed. Or writing one sentence in the document you've been avoiding. Or showing up to the gym, even if you don't feel like it. You don't need to feel motivated. You need to feel aligned with who you're becoming.

When Small Gets Big

Someone recently shared something honest and familiar. Every Monday, she told herself she would walk before work. Every week, she'd make it to Wednesday or Thursday and then stop. The routine would slide. And each time, her trust in herself took a little hit.

Eventually, she tried something smaller. Just one loop around the block. No gear. No tracking. No pressure. Seven days later, something shifted. She wasn't just walking. She was following through. By the second week, she was walking farther. Not because she had to but because she wanted to. That one block became a quiet, powerful message: I do what I say I will.

Most people focus on the goal, not the promise. They think, *I need to lose ten pounds* instead of *I'm walking today*. Behavioral science shows we're more likely to follow through when we connect actions to identity. The more we repeat something, the stronger that identity becomes.

So this week, don't make it about results. Make it about movement. Pick one small promise to keep. Keep it for yourself. And notice what happens when you prove you can.

The Fast Path to Keeping Your Word

1. Identify one small commitment you've broken repeatedly.
Nothing huge. Just something real.

2. Reframe it as a promise instead of a goal.
Something like "I make my bed every morning" or "I pause before I react." This subtle shift reinforces consistency over outcome.

3. Tell someone about it.
Not for affirmation. Let them know you're committing to this as part of showing up better in your life. Just saying it out loud creates a sense of intention, and sometimes, that's all you need to take it seriously.

4. Keep it for seven days.
Every time you do, say to yourself, "I follow through." This simple phrase reinforces identity and builds internal momentum. If you slip, don't worry. Just restart. Each day is a new chance to prove what you're capable of.

The Awareness Path to Rebuilding Trust
You can't rebuild trust in yourself overnight. But you don't need to. You just need one good week of following through to remember what it feels like. And that's enough to start believing again. I know that I believe in you.

Your What If Action

This week I will

45.

WHAT IF THIS WEEK, YOU ASKED SOMEONE YOU RESPECT FOR HONEST FEEDBACK?

A friend of mine once got some unexpected feedback from a work colleague. It wasn't requested. It wasn't helpful. And it definitely wasn't kind. It was delivered under the banner of just being honest, but it was more about the other person feeling threatened than it was about helping my friend grow.

That's the thing about most unsolicited feedback. It usually serves the person giving it more than the one receiving it. It comes with mixed motives, off timing, or no context. No wonder we get defensive. It often feels like an ambush.

However, when you intentionally invite feedback from someone you trust, the entire dynamic shifts; it becomes a tool, not a weapon—a mirror, not a magnifying glass.

And when you ask the right person in the right way, the response might surprise you. You might discover strengths you've been downplaying. Or you might hear something you already knew but needed to finally face. Either way, it gives you something to work with.

Invited feedback is a gift. And it's a risk worth taking.

Please Pass the Feedback

Most people wait until feedback shows up on a performance review, in a tense conversation, or during a moment of conflict. But that's like trying to steer a car after you've already hit the guardrail.

Inviting feedback allows you to learn on your terms. You get to choose the voice. You get to choose the timing. You get to lead the growth.

You're not asking for critique. You're asking for clarity. And that takes courage.

When you seek feedback, you're not trying to get it right; you're trying to improve. You're trying to get more aligned. You want to know how your actions land, how your presence is felt. What strengths should you keep leaning into, and where might you be holding yourself back?

So Let Me Ask

One of the simplest ways to open this up is to ask three specific questions:

What's something you think I do well that I might not even notice?
What's something I could improve that would make a real difference?
What's the one thing you believe would help me grow to my next level?

These questions don't just invite input. They open up a real conversation.

Most people who avoid feedback aren't afraid of being

criticized. They're fearful of being misunderstood, judged, or seen differently. However, the truth is that the longer you avoid feedback, the harder it becomes to grow. Not because you can't but because you're guessing instead of asking.

The Fast Path to Meaningful Feedback

1. Choose one person whose opinion you genuinely respect.
This could be a friend, partner, sibling, peer, manager, colleague, or mentor.

2. Let them know you're intentionally asking for honest insight, not evaluation or judgment.
Frame it as seeking growth, not evaluation. Let them know you genuinely want their honest perspective.

3. Ask the three questions above.
Be present. Listen fully—no interrupting or defending.

4. Reflect on what they share and decide how to use it.
Thank the person and take time to process what you heard. Decide which insights to act on and how.

The Awareness Path to Receiving Input
This week, notice your natural reaction to feedback—whether it's invited or not. Do you get defensive? Dismiss it? Overthink it? What if the real power isn't in accepting or rejecting feedback but rather in choosing when and how you seek it? Growth comes not just from knowing more but from being willing to ask the right people the right questions.

Your What If Action

This week I will _____

_____

_____

_____

_____

_____

_____

_____

_____

_____

_____

_____

_____

_____

_____

_____

_____

_____

_____

46.

WHAT IF THIS WEEK, YOU REDIRECTED YOUR THINKING WHEN IT GOES SOMEWHERE UNHELPFUL?

It sounds like a small thing. But it might be one of the most powerful What If shifts you can make.

I'm a stickler for being on time. My daughters would say that my version of "on time" is what most people consider early. When I'm on my own, it's easy. But when other humans are involved, it gets trickier.

I've noticed a pattern. The moment I feel like we're going to be late—even if there's no actual arrival time, just one I made up in my head—my thoughts start to race. I start thinking, *Maybe I should honk the horn. Perhaps I should remind them to put their shoes on earlier next time.* I feel myself getting edgy.

But none of that is helpful. And most of it isn't even necessary.

That's when I have to redirect my thinking. It's not about ignoring the feeling. It's about catching it, stepping back, and choosing a more useful path forward. One that keeps the peace, respects the people I'm with, and keeps me aligned with who I want to be.

When Your Brain Goes Rogue

You're going about your day, and something shifts. A comment. A mess. A delay. A headline. Your mind jumps in to make sense of it, predict it, fix it, or fight it. Sometimes those thoughts are helpful. But often, they spin out.

This isn't about pretending everything is fine. It's about shifting your attention toward something more grounded, more constructive, and more helpful to who you want to be in that moment.

Redirecting your thinking isn't about ignoring reality or forcing positivity. It's about deciding what kind of thinking you want to reinforce. It's a habit of pausing long enough to ask yourself, *Is this thought helping me right now?*

Most people who struggle with their thoughts try to force them to stop. They fight them or pretend they're not happening. But fighting thoughts usually makes them stronger. Redirecting is different. It's a gentle pivot toward something more useful.

The Second Thought Is Yours

Your first thought might be frustration, blame, or even panic. That's normal. That's human. But your next thought? That's up to you.

The coworker who's always late with something you need. The traffic that's making you later than you wanted to be. The dishwasher that still isn't empty, despite having asked someone twice. Your brain offers up the first reaction automatically. But you get to choose what comes next.

A helpful way to start is to label the moment for what it is. "My thoughts are racing." "I'm jumping to conclusions." "I'm replaying something that already happened." That simple act of naming it gives you distance.

Then, instead of judging the thought or trying to shut it down, get curious. Ask yourself, *What's a better thought here?* or *What would I tell someone else in this situation?*

The goal isn't perfect positivity. The goal is useful thinking.

The Fast Path to Redirecting Your Thoughts

1. Catch the thought.
Notice when your thinking starts to spiral, judge, or catastrophize. Don't fight it. Just name it.

2. Ask yourself, Is this helpful right now?
If not, it's time to shift.

3. Redirect yourself with a better question.
Something like "What else might be true?" or "What do I want to feel instead?" or "What's the best way I can respond?"

4. Reinforce it with action.
It could be a deep breath. A kind word. A calm response. Even a simple pause. The action tells your brain the new direction is real.

The Awareness Path to Choosing Your Second Thought
Your thoughts will wander this week—that's normal. What matters is recognizing when they've gone somewhere unhelpful and gently guiding them back. You can't control every first thought, but you can control which ones you follow. Each time you catch yourself spiraling and choose a better

direction, you're strengthening your ability to think in ways that serve you.

Your What If Action

This week I will _____

_____

_____

_____

_____

_____

_____

_____

_____

_____

_____

_____

47.

WHAT IF THIS WEEK, YOU PRACTICED DISAGREEING BETTER?

When Phil Jackson took over coaching the Chicago Bulls, he inherited one of the most unconventional players the NBA has ever seen: Dennis Rodman.

Usually sporting wild, colored hair, Rodman was explosive, emotional, and unpredictable. He clashed with the media, bent team rules, and often lived in chaos off the court. Most coaches would have tried to fix him or get rid of him altogether.

But Jackson didn't. He disagreed with a lot of Rodman's behavior, but he didn't make the disagreement personal. Instead, he worked to understand him. He learned what motivated him, what grounded him, and how to create boundaries without stripping away Rodman's individuality.

Rodman, in return, gave Jackson everything on the court. He played with discipline, intensity, and commitment. He was one of the best rebounders in the game. And together, they won championships.

That story has stayed with me. Because it's not only about basketball and coaching—it's about how we handle disagreement.

Some people push too hard in conflict. Others avoid it altogether. Most of us do a little of both, depending on the moment. But either way, we often treat disagreement like a problem to fix or a battle to win.

You Don't Have to Dye Your Hair to Disagree

Disagreement isn't failure. It's friction. And friction, handled well, can shape something better.

Disagreeing better means knowing when to speak and how to speak. It means having the awareness to see if you're being principled or just reactive. It means recognizing that you can hold your view without dismissing someone else's.

If you're someone who argues quickly, ask yourself: *Am I trying to protect my point, or am I trying not to be wrong or to shut down the conversation?*

If you're someone who stays silent, ask: *What part of me is afraid to speak up, and what's the cost of that silence?*

You don't have to avoid disagreement this week. You don't have to win it either. You just have to handle it better. With more presence, more calm, and more connection.

Your Conflict Signature

Some people avoid conflict because it makes them anxious or unsure of what to say. Others step in too quickly, trying to control the moment before it turns messy.

If you tend to argue quickly or forcefully, start by slowing your response. Let silence do some of the work. Ask a question before offering your opinion. You'll come across as more grounded and more respectful when you don't overpower the moment.

If you tend to shrink or stay quiet, remember that disagreement isn't about creating tension. It's about showing up. Start with a simple phrase, such as, "Can I offer another way to look at this?" or "I see it a little differently." The more you practice, the more natural it becomes.

Disagreement doesn't have to break the connection. Learning to disagree better can strengthen it. And sometimes, the best resolution is no resolution at all. Agreeing to disagree isn't a sign of giving up. It's giving the relationship more room than the argument.

The Fast Path to Grounded Disagreement

1. Pause before reacting or retreating.

Ask the values question: What matters most here—being right, being heard, or being real?

2. Start with calm clarity.

If you tend to argue, slow down and ask a question first. If you tend to shrink, try a simple opener like "Can I share another perspective?"

3. Stay anchored in values.

Speak from your principles, not your emotions. Focus on what matters, not on what stings.

4. End with connection, not control.

Whether you agree or not, try to close with respect: "Thank you for sharing your idea."

The Awareness Path to Understanding Your Conflict Style
Think back to a disagreement where you argued too much or said too little. What were you feeling in that moment— defensive, anxious, unsure, frustrated? What were you trying to protect—your position, your peace, your place? This week, pay attention to those moments and notice your patterns.

Your What If Action

This week I will

48.

WHAT IF THIS WEEK, YOU CAUGHT YOUR ATTITUDE BEFORE IT CAUGHT YOU?

I once yelled at my kids to stop yelling. How ironic, huh? The moment the words came out of my mouth, I knew I had become the energy I was trying to change. That's how fast an attitude can flip and how easy it is to pass it along without meaning to.

We all know how it happens. You spill your coffee. Get stuck in traffic. Get an email that sets you off. Now the mood isn't just a moment. It's running the show. What started as a bad five minutes becomes a bad attitude, a bad interaction, a bad day.

Most people think moods are fixed. But they're fluid. Moods are contagious. Good and bad. They feed on attention and repetition. The shift happens not because we feel bad but because we give that feeling authority over everything else. The earlier you catch it, the easier it is to turn around.

That's the What If Rule in action. Pause. Reframe. Choose a better perspective and option. Not to deny what happened but to avoid giving it more power than it deserves.

The Mood Snowball
Research shows that your mood tends to continue in the

direction it's already heading, unless something interrupts it. Scientists call this emotional inertia—once you're rolling downhill, you pick up speed. But here's the good news: Even small physical or verbal changes can shift emotional states. That's why catching it early matters. The longer a negative mood rolls, the more momentum it builds.

The key isn't to be relentlessly positive. It's to be emotionally agile.

Operation Mood Flip

Here's the moment most people miss: When your attitude starts to go sideways, your brain wants to double down. You feel justified. You replay what went wrong. But what if you interrupted the spiral with something that feels almost too simple?

Stand up. Roll your shoulders back. Take one deep breath. Smile—even a half smile. Then say something encouraging out loud: "All right, time for a U-turn."

It sounds ridiculous. But your body and brain are wired to respond to physical and verbal cues. When you change your posture, you're literally changing your chemistry. When you smile, even a forced one, your brain releases feel-good chemicals. When you speak encouragement out loud, you're interrupting the negative internal dialogue. That ten-second reset often creates just enough space to stop the slide.

You don't need to fix your whole day. You just need to stop the momentum. And remember this: You can start your day over at any time. One new moment, one different choice— that's all it takes to turn things around.

And if part of turning things around means apologizing, do it. Not just for the other person but for you. Owning the moment helps you move forward. Saying you're sorry doesn't mean you're wrong. It just means you're sorry it happened. That's clarity, not weakness.

The Fast Path to Attitude Reset

1. Catch your attitude early.
Notice when you feel off, irritable, or closed down. Don't wait for someone else to call it out. Catch the shift before it becomes the tone of the day.

2. Name the shift.
Think: *I'm starting to go there. I can choose something different.* Giving it language gives you power.

3. Do one small opposite action.
Break your posture. Smile at someone. Say thank you. Let someone go in traffic. Take a short walk. Interrupt the energy physically and relationally.

4. Ask yourself: Do I need to start my day over?
It doesn't matter the time of day or what's going on. You can always choose to make the attitude U-turn and start your day over.

The Awareness Path to Catching Your Mood Early
Pay attention to how easily minor frustrations can shape your entire mood. Notice the moment when something small starts to color everything else. What would it feel like to catch that shift earlier and make a different choice on purpose? You don't

have to control every mood, but you don't have to surrender to every one either.

Your What If Action

This week I will _____

_____

_____

_____

_____

_____

_____

_____

_____

_____

_____

_____

ATTRACTION, NOT PROMOTION

A Change & Growth Inflection Chapter

When you start to change and grow, it's natural to want the people around you to join in. You feel better. You're learning something new. You see a shift happening, and it's exciting. Of course you want others to experience it too.

But that excitement can backfire if you're not careful.

I remember when I first got serious about eating healthier. I was all in. I was reading about nutrition, trying new foods, and learning how certain things affected energy and focus. I felt great, and I wanted everyone else to feel great too.

So I did what a lot of people do. I started pointing things out.

That's not good for you. You know what's in that, right? You really should try what I'm doing.

Shockingly, no one was thrilled. Instead of feeling inspired, they felt judged. Instead of joining me, they shut down.

Looking back, I get it. I wasn't being helpful. I was being pushy. I wasn't leading by example; I was correcting. I had forgotten something we used to tell our daughters all the time when they were younger:

Don't yuck someone else's yum.

It's true for food, and it's true for change. Most people aren't motivated by pressure. They're motivated by possibility. And the best way to show them the possibility is to live it. You don't have to convince them. You don't have to debate them. You don't have to fix them.

Just keep showing up.

You can encourage others, of course. You can share what's helping you. You can offer resources, give someone a copy of this book, or talk openly about how good it feels to grow.

But at the end of the day, the most powerful influence isn't what you tell people.

It's what they see in you.

Change is contagious, but not when it's forced. The goal is attraction, not promotion. Let your life be the invitation.

That's the kind of example people want to follow.

49.

WHAT IF THIS WEEK, WHEN SOMETHING ISN'T GOING RIGHT, YOU LEANED IN AND LEARNED FROM IT?

Most people label situations as bad the moment they feel uncomfortable.

A meeting goes sideways. A plan falls apart. You burn something in the oven. A report you're working on crashes.

Something minor turns messy. Before you've even finished reacting, your brain assigns it meaning: wrong, frustrating, disappointing.

But what if that moment wasn't only those things?

What if it was a growth moment in disguise?

Not a punishment. Not a sign you failed. Just a real-life reminder that something might need your attention. Something might be shifting. Something might even be trying to help you.

Every difficult moment is a fork in the road. You can resist it, or you can learn from it. That one shift changes everything.

The Happy Accident Hall of Fame
In the early 1990s, researchers at Pfizer were testing a new drug designed to treat chest pain from heart disease. The

medication was called sildenafil. But during clinical trials, something unexpected happened. The drug didn't help chest pain, yet the men in the study refused to return their pills.

Researchers discovered that sildenafil had a very different effect than expected. The drug that failed in its original purpose became something entirely different. Today, that drug is known as Viagra.

Nobody set out to invent it. But someone noticed what wasn't going right and leaned in anyway.

It's a perfect example of how reframing what's not working can lead to a completely different and sometimes better result. You don't have to be a scientist to use that mindset. You just have to stop assuming that when things don't go as planned, they've gone wrong.

You Choose the Meaning

Here's what most people don't realize: Everything that happens is neutral until you assign it meaning. The same moment can be frustrating and formative. The frustration doesn't cancel out growth—it can actually point toward it.

This doesn't mean pretending things are great when they're not. It means being honest enough to say, "This isn't ideal, but maybe there's something here for me to learn."

That pause and reframe doesn't erase the frustration. It simply adds purpose to it. You can feel what you feel and still grow from it. When you lean in with curiosity, you invite insight. When you resist, you get stuck.

Most people assume learning happens after the fact, when things have settled and the emotion has passed. And yes, sometimes that's true. But real growth occurs more quickly when you train yourself to adapt in the moment.

This week's shift is simple. When something isn't going right, pause your reaction. Label the moment as a learning opportunity. Then ask what you can take from it.

That alone changes how you experience what's hard. Instead of feeling thrown off, you'll feel more grounded. Instead of just getting through it, you'll come out of it with something useful.

The Fast Path to Finding the Lesson

1. Catch the trigger moment.
Notice when something feels off, frustrating, or disappointing. This is your cue to pause and determine whether there's something here you can learn or shift.

2. Label the moment as a learning opportunity.
It sounds too simple, but putting a name to it reorients your brain. You're no longer reacting, you're reflecting.

3. Ask yourself what the growth is here.
Is it patience? Better preparation? Clearer communication? Turn on autosave going forward? Set a timer. Find even a small takeaway.

4. Apply the lesson moving forward.
Learning doesn't end with insight. Use what you saw to make a different move next time. That's the real growth.

The Awareness Path to Growing Through It
This week, whenever something frustrates you or throws you

off, pause and name it. Not as a failure. Not as a setback. Just a learning moment. That pause, that label, that small act of curiosity—it shifts your entire experience. You won't just *get* through it. You'll *grow* through it.

Your What If Action

This week I will _____

_____

_____

_____

_____

_____

_____

_____

_____

_____

50.

WHAT IF THIS WEEK, YOU TOOK A MEANINGFUL RISK WORTH THE STRETCH?

I knew someone who had a good job but couldn't shake the feeling that he was supposed to be doing something else. For years, he talked about switching careers. But whenever it got serious, he'd shut it down.

It probably wouldn't work out.
I'd have to start over.
People like me don't get to do that.

Then one day, after nudges from a couple of us, he decided to put his résumé out there. No announcement. No big leap. Just one forward motion.

A few weeks later, he landed an interview. And in the process of preparing for the interview, talking with others, and learning more about the role, something shifted. He realized he didn't actually want the job. The version of his life he thought he was chasing didn't match who he'd become.

What he got from that small risk wasn't a new career. It was clarity. Confidence. A deeper appreciation for where he was.

Risk isn't always about change. It's often about clarity.

Not All Risks Require a Cape

Most people associate risk with disruption. Quitting the job, launching the business, and making the bold move. But real-world growth risks are usually smaller, subtler, and more personal.

They're the conversations you almost don't start. The ideas you almost don't share. The opportunities you nearly don't explore.

And they're often the exact thing that shows you what you're capable of or what matters.

Like asking someone you respect to be your mentor. You risk being told no or, worse, being ignored completely. But more often, the risk reveals that people are far more open to helping than we assume. The upside isn't just their guidance. It's the confidence you gain from making the ask in the first place.

Like getting on a dating app after a tough breakup. You risk feeling exposed, judged, or ghosted. But the bigger risk is believing your story is already written. Sometimes the boldest risk is simply allowing for the possibility that something good could still be ahead.

What about exploring a part-time gig? The risk isn't just failure. It's what people might think. What if it doesn't work? What if it's a waste of time? But taking a step forward might give you what years of thinking never could: real insight, real momentum, and maybe even a new direction.

These aren't wild moves. They're courageous ones. And they're how real life opens up.

The Beautiful Awkwardness of Trying

When considering a stretch or change, most people tend to focus on what could go wrong. But real growth often comes from doing something simply to see what it reveals.

You're not committing to a full leap. You're just taking a step to learn. The discomfort isn't a warning sign. It's part of the process. Acting before you're certain is how you build clarity, confidence, and next steps.

The Fast Path to Taking the Risk

1. Think of something you've been wondering about but haven't acted on.

A shift. A conversation. An opportunity. A "maybe someday" you keep circling back to.

2. Identify one small step that would move it forward.

Not a leap. Just a move that makes it real.

3. Remind yourself that risk isn't a promise.

It's a permission. You're allowed to find out, even if the answer is no.

4. Take the step this week and learn from what happens next.

It may turn into something big. It might not work out at all. Either way, you'll learn something valuable.

The Awareness Path to Moving Forward

This week, take note of where you're hesitating, not out of logic but out of fear. Ask yourself what you might gain by moving forward just a little. The best way to stop overthinking is to start learning. And learning usually begins with risk.

Your What If Action

This week I will _____

_____

_____

_____

_____

_____

_____

_____

_____

_____

_____

51.

WHAT IF THIS WEEK, YOU WERE QUICKER TO ADMIT WHEN YOU WERE WRONG OR MISTAKEN?

For many years, I would never admit when I was wrong.

I'd argue my way through a mistake. I'd deny it. I'd deflect it. Not because I thought I was always right but because I was afraid of what being wrong said about me.

At the time, I didn't realize that fear was rooted in feeling like I didn't measure up to other people. I didn't want anyone to see how unsure I felt inside. So if I admitted I was wrong, I worried that everyone would see just how inferior I was.

It wasn't about the mistake. It was about the meaning I gave it.

As I grew older and more confident, that started to shift. I began to see myself not as better or worse than anyone else but as equally human. Still, I often delayed owning my missteps. I didn't lie—but I hesitated. I'd smooth it over. Stay vague. Or move on without saying the words out loud.

What finally changed me was recovery and the practice of regularly taking personal inventory. That's how I learned one of the most underrated truths about growth: Being wrong is normal. Owning it is powerful.

You might already be good at this. Not everyone struggles with admitting when they're wrong. However, most of us hesitate to own our mistakes or misunderstandings at some point.

This week is about catching yourself sooner when you do hesitate, not with guilt but with self-awareness and the strength to say, "That one's on me."

The Weird Power of Being Wrong

Admitting a mistake doesn't make you weaker; it makes you stronger.

When I reached a point where I could admit I was wrong without shame, I unlocked something far more valuable: the ability to learn. I became someone others could trust more. I started building better relationships more quickly. And I became more confident, not less, because I wasn't afraid of what being wrong said about me anymore.

Most people think credibility comes from always being right. But it comes from how you handle being wrong. The person who can say "I missed that" or "You're right" without defensiveness? That's someone people want to work with, live with, and trust.

The Two-Second Trust Builder

The fastest way to build trust isn't being perfect—it's being honest about imperfection in real time.

When you quickly admit a mistake, several things happen: You stop the cycle of defensiveness that kills conversations. You model the kind of honesty that makes others feel safe to be honest too. And you free yourself from the exhausting job of pretending you never make a mistake.

This becomes even more powerful when children are watching. Kids learn more from what they see than what they're told. When they watch you admit a mistake without drama or shame, you're teaching them that being human is OK. That mistakes don't define you, but how you handle them does. That's a lesson that will serve them for life—and it starts with you showing them how it's done.

The Fast Path to Owning Your Mistakes

1. Notice the urge to deflect.
Catch the moment when you want to explain away, minimize, or say nothing at all. That's your signal to lean in instead of pull back.

2. Say it simply and clearly.
"You're right, I missed that." "That was my mistake." "I was wrong about that." Don't bury the ownership in explanations or excuses.

3. Let the moment land without fixing it.
Resist the urge to justify or overexplain. Give the other person space to process your honesty. Most people respect ownership more than perfection.

4. Move forward without carrying shame.
Being wrong about something doesn't make you wrong as a person. Learn from it, then let it go. That's how ownership becomes a source of strength instead of weakness.

The Awareness Path to Quick Ownership

At some point this week, you might feel that twinge—the one that says, "I was off there." Don't push past it. Pause and ask yourself: *What if I just admitted it?* See what happens when you stop protecting your ego and start protecting the relationship and your growth.

Your What If Action

This week I will _____

_____

_____

_____

_____

_____

_____

_____

_____

52.

WHAT IF THIS WEEK, FROM TIME TO TIME, YOU JUST MOVED ON?

Our dog Piper always has to get the last word. She'll bark at something outside, and when told to stop, she does. Kind of. There's always one last little noise. A soft grumble or a breathy half bark. Just enough to make her opinion known. Every time it happens I tell her to stop. Then my wife laughs and says the same thing: "Just move on." And she's right. It's such a simple idea, but it's not always easy to do.

Someone makes a snarky comment, and we feel the urge to fire one back. Someone's wrong on the internet, and we're suddenly writing a reply. We think of something clever we could have said earlier, and we rehearse it in our minds as if we still need to win the moment. But what if the real strength wasn't in finishing the argument? What if it was in stepping away from it?

I once watched two men in a meeting go from a calm discussion to a heated argument in under five minutes. Initially, it was merely a difference of opinion. Then the tone shifted. The volume rose. Neither one was willing to back down. One person finally stormed out and never returned to the meeting. That moment stuck with me. I call it the escalation effect—when something small grows into something big simply because no one chooses to step away from it.

The Last-Word Syndrome
Escalation doesn't just happen in arguments. It happens in our minds. It happens in our emotions. One small thing hits us wrong, and we carry it into the next hour. A moment of annoyance turns into an afternoon of frustration. A text with the wrong tone ruins a night that hadn't even started yet.

Escalation is what turns something small into something heavy. It creates pressure where there is no need for it. It's the little fire that keeps growing because we keep adding oxygen.

Here's what most people don't realize: The other person usually isn't even thinking about it anymore. The friction stays alive in us, not them. We're fighting a battle they've already forgotten about.

That's where the power of moving on comes in. It's not weakness. It's not pretending something didn't happen. It's simply about choosing to protect your energy, time, and day. It's saying, "I don't need to finish this fight. I don't need the last word. I don't need to carry this forward."

When Moving On Is Moving Up
A friend of mine shared a moment that changed how she handles conflict. She was in a heated text exchange with her sister. Each message was a little more defensive than the last. She found herself typing longer and longer responses, trying to make her point clearer.

Then she stopped. She looked at what she'd written and

realized she was about to send three paragraphs explaining why she was right about something that happened five years ago. She deleted the message and wrote instead: "You know what? I love you. Let's talk about something else."

Her sister responded immediately: "Thank you. I love you too."

That was it. No more tension. No lingering resentment. Just two people who chose connection over being right.

Moving on isn't giving up. It's choosing what matters more. And most of the time, what matters more is the relationship, the peace, or simply having a good day.

The Fast Path to Moving On

1. Notice the moment it starts.
When your body tenses, your mind loops, or your words speed up—stop. That's your cue that something is building.

2. Decide how far you want this to go.
Is it worth your time? Your peace? Your day? Most of the time, it's not. Say that clearly to yourself.

3. Choose your exit move.
Take a breath, change the subject, or physically step away. Find your healthy way out of the moment.

4. Move forward.
Don't carry the tension with you. Don't replay the moment over and over. Let moving on be the strength you lead with.

The Awareness Path to Catching Escalation Early

This week, notice the small moments that try to pull you in. The comment that irritates you. The urge to correct someone. The mental replay of something from the past. Pay attention to how escalation starts—usually with something tiny that grows because we feed it. Notice how good it feels when you catch it early and just move on instead.

Your What If Action

This week I will _____

_____

_____

_____

_____

_____

_____

_____

53.

WHAT IF THIS WEEK, YOU WENT ABOVE AND BEYOND FOR SOMEONE OR SOMETHING?

This book has fifty-three What If questions.

You probably expected fifty-two—one for each week of the year. That would have made sense. Would've been enough.

But this is the bonus chapter. The one you didn't plan for. The one you didn't need to finish the book. The one that goes a little beyond what was expected.

And that's the point.

Sometimes the most meaningful actions are the ones no one asks for. The thank-you note that didn't have to be written. The follow-up call that wasn't required. The time you stayed longer, listened deeper, or showed up stronger, just because you could.

This week's What If is about doing more than necessary. Not to prove anything. Not to be the hero. But because a little extra, done with intention, can leave a lasting mark.

The Extra Step

Life is built better in the extra step. The kind word when someone didn't expect one. The follow-through that shows you care. The above-and-beyond action that makes someone's day, not just your deadline.

When you choose to do more, it affects people. It shapes the atmosphere around you. It lifts the bar without needing to say a word.

I call it Give to Get. You give more, not to be noticed but to get more of the world you want to live in. That could be a more positive home. A more respectful workplace. A moment that brings someone joy. When you go above and beyond, you help create the kind of energy and experience you hope others would create for you.

The Fast Path to Above and Beyond

1. Choose someone or something that matters.
Pick a person, a project, or a space in your world that could use a little unexpected care.

2. Decide what "extra" looks like this time.
It could be time, effort, kindness, clarity, or support. You get to define it.

3. Do it with zero strings attached.
This isn't about recognition. It's about showing up fully—because that's who you are.

4. Notice what comes back.

You'll likely feel it. A better energy. A lifted mood. A connection made stronger. The Get is often quiet, but it's real.

The Awareness Path to More of What Matters

At some point this week, you'll feel like you've done enough. And maybe you have. But if you sense there's just a little more in you to give, give it. Not out of pressure. Out of choice. One extra step can shift a moment, a relationship, or even a room.

Your What If Action

This week I will

SHOW UP FOR YOU

A Change & Growth Inflection Chapter

Self-worth is a tricky topic, although it's a crucial aspect of personal change and growth.

After I got into recovery, I hated talking about self-worth. The term made me flinch. It felt like ego. Or self-centeredness. Or something soft and syrupy, like one of those mirror affirmations: "You're good enough, you're smart enough . . ." You know the rest.

But eventually, I had to face something I couldn't keep ignoring: I couldn't give what I didn't have.

I couldn't offer real love or presence to others until I started being OK with myself. I couldn't bring joy into a room if I wasn't open to joy. I couldn't be fully there for others when I was quietly tearing myself apart inside. It wasn't about boosting my ego. It was about getting grounded enough inside that I had something real to give.

That's when self-worth stopped feeling like self-centered sappiness and started feeling like service. The kind that begins when you're solid enough in who you are to show up with something meaningful to offer.

You don't have to feel amazing about yourself all the time. You don't have to chant mantras or radiate positivity. But you do have to believe you're worth the effort. Worth the changes. Worth the process. Not because you've proven anything but because you matter. And because becoming more is always possible when you believe you deserve to.

So no, I'm not asking you to look in the mirror and say, "Gosh darn it, people like me."

But I am reminding you:

You're worthy of the goodness the world has to offer.

And the goodness you have to offer the world.

WHAT IF THIS IS NOT THE END BUT JUST THE BEGINNING?

Whether you've worked through every weekly chapter or just absorbed the concepts, you now understand how a simple shift in thinking can create new perspectives and options.

The real power of the What If Rule isn't in following a structured weekly format forever. It's in developing the instinct to pause and ask better questions whenever life presents you with a choice, a challenge, or an opportunity. The goal is to become someone who naturally sees possibilities where others see problems and who spots opportunities when others don't.

Making What If Thinking Automatic

The transition from practicing What If questions to living What If thinking happens gradually, then suddenly. One day, you'll realize you're automatically asking, "What if there's another way to see this?" when you feel frustrated. Or, "What if this setback is redirecting me toward something better?" when plans fall apart. Or, "What if I approached this conversation differently?" before walking into a difficult meeting.

This shift happens faster when you intentionally use What If questions in your daily decisions. Don't wait for a perfect moment or reflection time—make it part of how you move through your day. Ask "What if I tried something new today?" when choosing your route to work. Try "What if I listened more than I talked?" before important conversations. Use "What if this could be easier?" when tasks feel overwhelming.

The more contexts you apply the What If Rule, the more natural it becomes to see multiple perspectives and options instead of getting stuck in single-track thinking. Eventually, it stops being something you do and starts being how you think.

Sharing What If with Others

As this approach becomes part of how you navigate life, people will notice. They'll see you responding to stress with curiosity instead of reactivity. They'll watch you find creative solutions when others feel stuck.

When they ask what's different, you'll have a simple answer: "I've learned to ask better questions."

As you learned in the Attraction, Not Promotion chapter, the most powerful way to share What If thinking is through example, not explanation. Use What If questions in conversations with family, friends, and colleagues. Instead of giving advice, ask, "What if you tried approaching this differently?" Instead of solving problems for others, ask, "What if there's something we're not seeing here?"

People follow what they see working, not what they're told should work.

Keep Evolving and Growing

The journey of change and growth never really ends. There's always another level of possibility to explore, another area of life where What If thinking can create breakthroughs.

Join my newsletter to continue receiving fresh What If questions and insights that keep you growing.

And if you'd like to work with me through some bigger personal or business What If challenges and opportunities, I offer The What If Breakthrough™ Coaching.

For more resources, speaking opportunities, and ways to deepen your What If practice, visit dougfleener.com.

Your Road Ahead

I'm excited for what's ahead for you. As I mentioned before, we act our way into a new way of thinking—and once your thinking shifts, everything else follows. A richer, better life comes from that simple cycle. Just follow three easy steps: Pause. Question. Go.

You're one action away. Starting today.

With peace and love,
Doug Fleener

APPENDIX: THE WHAT IF RULE IN ACTION

The following sections focus on applying the What If Rule in specific life situations. They show how the same approach you've been practicing can create better outcomes in work, relationships, health, finances, and more.

You don't need to read these sections in order. Jump to the areas that are most relevant to you right now. The more areas of your life you apply the What If Rule, the more natural it becomes to see more and different perspectives and options. One simple approach—Pause. Question. Go.—works everywhere you choose to use it.

What if this becomes the way you approach every area of your life?

THE WHAT IF RULE IN ACTION: AT WORK

Your work environment is full of untapped possibilities. Whether you're an individual contributor looking to enhance your performance, a team leader building stronger relationships, or an executive creating new opportunities, What If questions can transform how you approach your professional life.

The beauty of this approach is that it works at every level—from daily interactions with colleagues to strategic planning sessions. You don't need permission or a title to start using What If thinking. You just need the willingness to see your current situation through a lens of possibility rather than limitation.

Reframe challenges and frustrations.
When you encounter a difficult situation, ask, "What if there's something I'm not seeing here?" or "What if I approached this completely differently?" This shift often reveals solutions hidden by habit or frustration. Instead of getting pulled into "this always happens" thinking, you open yourself to creative alternatives that can break through long-standing obstacles.

Make strategic decisions.
Before important choices, ask, "What if I considered this from my customer's perspective?" or "What if there are long-term implications I haven't considered?" Better questions lead to better decisions. Taking time to explore different angles

prevents reactive choices and helps you see opportunities that might otherwise be missed. It's also a great way to test final decisions.

Improve communication and collaboration.

When conversations feel tense or unproductive, try asking, "What if they have a valid point I'm missing?" or "What if we're trying to solve the same problem?" This shifts you from a defensive to a curious mindset, often uncovering common ground that moves projects forward and strengthens working relationships.

Create new opportunities.

Ask, "What if I took the lead on this project?" or "What if I shared my expertise more openly?" These questions help you discover growth and visibility opportunities that already exist in your role—no more waiting for opportunities to be handed to you. What If thinking enables you to create them.

Enhance what's already working.

Look at successful processes and ask, "What if we could make this even better?" or "What if we applied this approach to other areas?" The best improvements often come from building on existing strengths, not just fixing problems.

The What If workplace is full of possibilities and new opportunities.

THE WHAT IF RULE IN ACTION: RELATIONSHIPS

Relationships thrive on connection, understanding, and growth—but they often get stuck in patterns of reaction and assumption.

Whether you're navigating marriage, friendship, family dynamics, or dating, What If questions can transform how you connect with the people who matter most. Instead of defaulting to familiar responses or getting caught in cycles of misunderstanding, you can use What If thinking to create deeper connections and stronger bonds.

Reframe reactive patterns.
When you feel yourself getting triggered or defensive, pause and ask, "What if they're not trying to hurt me?" or "What if this reaction says more about my day than about them?" This simple shift can prevent arguments from escalating and help you respond from a place of clarity rather than emotion.

Shift tension into curiosity.
During disagreements, try asking, "What if we're both right about different parts of this?" or "What if there's something I'm missing about their perspective?" These questions move you away from being right toward being connected, often revealing common ground you didn't see before.

Stay open to possibility in difficult moments.
When relationships feel strained, ask, "What if this rough patch is bringing us closer?" or "What if working through this makes us stronger?" This perspective helps you see challenges as opportunities for growth rather than threats to the relationship. It also keeps the focus on the way forward over getting stuck where you are.

Choose presence over routine.
In everyday interactions, ask, "What if I gave them my full attention right now?" or "What if I were more intentional in this moment?" These questions help you break free from distracted, surface-level connections and create the kind of presence that deepens relationships.

Create new possibilities for connection.
Look for opportunities to enhance good relationships by asking, "What if we tried something new together?" or "What if I expressed appreciation more often?" The strongest relationships are built through intentional choices, not just shared history.

The What If relationship is built on curiosity, presence, and the willingness to see new possibilities.

THE WHAT IF RULE IN ACTION: LEADERSHIP

Whether you're leading a team of two or an organization of thousands, the What If Rule can transform how you lead, inspire, and grow your people and your results.

Great leaders understand that their role isn't to solve every problem but rather to create an environment where solutions emerge. Asking What If questions helps you do precisely that, fostering ownership, creativity, and growth in the people you lead while strengthening your leadership effectiveness.

Accelerate organizational growth and results.

Challenge your team with strategic questions, such as, "What if we could double our donations in the next quarter?" or "What if we eliminated our biggest bottleneck within 30 days?" These questions push beyond incremental improvements to breakthrough thinking that drives rapid organizational advancement.

Coach your team using What If questions.

Instead of jumping straight to solutions, ask, "What if we approached this challenge differently?" or "What if you had unlimited resources—what would you try?" This approach develops your team's problem-solving abilities while demonstrating your trust in their judgment. It transforms you from a problem solver to a problem-solving catalyst.

Encourage ownership and accountability.

When others bring you problems, try asking, "What if you were in my position—what would you recommend?" or "What if this were your company—how would you handle it?" These questions shift responsibility back to them while demonstrating confidence in their capabilities and judgment.

Use What If in team meetings to inspire new ideas.

Transform routine meetings by asking, "What if we could improve this process by 50 percent?" or "What if our current approach didn't limit us?" This fosters psychological safety for bold thinking and often uncovers innovative solutions that structured brainstorming sessions may overlook.

Stretch thinking without being directive.

Guide development by asking, "What if you took on more visibility in this area?" or "What if this setback is preparation for something bigger?" You're planting seeds for growth rather than mandating specific actions, which creates more authentic buy-in.

Effective leadership is about helping others discover their own answers and leadership through the power of What If.

THE WHAT IF RULE IN ACTION: PARENTING

Parenting is one of the most challenging and rewarding places to practice the What If Rule. Whether you're raising toddlers, teenagers, or anything in between, What If questions can transform everyday moments into opportunities for growth, connection, and learning.

Instead of falling into reactive patterns or power struggles, you can use What If thinking to guide your children toward independence while strengthening your relationship with them.

Turn mistakes into learning moments.

When your child makes a poor choice, instead of immediately jumping to consequences, try asking, "What if we figured out what happened here?" or "What if you could handle this differently next time?" This approach teaches problem-solving skills while demonstrating that mistakes are growth opportunities, not just reasons for punishment.

Encourage independence and critical thinking.

Rather than solving every problem for them, ask, "What if you tried to work this out first?" or "What if there's a solution you haven't thought of yet?" These questions build confidence and decision-making abilities while demonstrating trust in the child's judgment and capability.

Use What If to open difficult conversations.

When addressing sensitive topics, try asking, "What if we talked about what's going on?" or "What if you could tell me anything without getting in trouble?" This creates psychological safety and often leads to more honest communication than direct questioning.

Help them navigate social challenges.

When they're struggling with friends or school situations, ask, "What if they're dealing with something difficult too?" or "What if you approached this person differently?" This fosters empathy and equips them with tools for navigating relationships throughout their lives.

Build resilience through perspective.

During disappointments or setbacks, try asking, "What if this teaches you something important?" or "What if this leads to something even better?" You're not dismissing their feelings but rather helping them develop the ability to see challenges as part of growth, not just as obstacles.

The What If parent raises children who can better navigate life's challenges and opportunities.

THE WHAT IF RULE IN ACTION:
BUSINESS OWNERSHIP

Owning a business, regardless of its size, demands constant decision-making, strategic thinking, and the ability to identify opportunities that others miss. Whether you're running a start-up, scaling an established company, or navigating market changes, What If questions can transform how you approach growth, leadership, and balance.

Instead of getting caught in the day-to-day grind or feeling overwhelmed by complexity, you can use What If thinking to gain clarity and create breakthrough results.

Reimagine strategy and direction.

When your current approach feels stagnant or unclear, ask, "What if we wanted to double our size in three years?" or "What if this industry challenge could become our new competitive advantage?" These questions help you step back from tactical execution to see strategic possibilities you might have missed while being too close to the business.

Unlock new opportunities.

Look beyond your current offerings by asking, "What if our customers needed something we're not providing?" or "What if we could solve a problem no one else is addressing?" This perspective often reveals untapped revenue streams or market opportunities that were previously hidden in plain sight.

Navigate tough decisions with more confidence.
When facing difficult choices, try asking, "What if six months from now we realized it was the wrong decision?" or "What if we do nothing?" These questions help you move past analysis paralysis to make decisions aligned with your bigger goals.

Managing cash flow and financial decisions.
When facing financial pressures or investment choices, ask, "What if we looked at this decision six months from now?" or "What if the costs from this vendor go up by 25 percent next month?" These questions help you move beyond fear-based thinking to make strategic financial choices that support long-term growth rather than just short-term survival.

Create better work-life integration.
Challenge the assumption that business success requires personal sacrifice by asking, "What if I could grow the business while working less?" or "What if I could go away for a month?" This helps you design a business that serves your life, not the other way around.

The What If business owner builds companies that create value while enhancing life.

THE WHAT IF RULE IN ACTION: CAREER NAVIGATION AND JOB SEEKING

Career decisions can feel overwhelming, whether you're exploring new opportunities, considering a change, or actively searching for a job. What If questions can transform these pivotal moments from sources of stress into strategic advantages. Instead of making career moves based on fear, desperation, or limited thinking, you can use What If thinking to uncover hidden possibilities and make choices aligned with your long-term goals.

Clarify whether to stay, grow, or go.

When feeling stuck in your current role, ask, "What if I could re-create my job to fit what I want?" or "What if staying here for another year positioned me perfectly for my next move?" These questions help you see options beyond the simple stay-or-leave dilemma.

Accelerate advancement in your current position.

Instead of waiting for opportunities to come to you, ask, "What if I started taking on responsibilities above my current level?" or "What if I became the go-to person for solving this type of problem?" These questions help you create visibility and demonstrate readiness for advancement by actively seeking ways to add more value.

Reframe rejection and setbacks.

When facing job rejections or career disappointments, ask, "What if this is redirecting me toward something better?" or "What if this feedback contains the key to my next breakthrough?" These questions help you extract value from difficult experiences and shield you from getting discouraged.

Prepare for interviews and important conversations.

Instead of just rehearsing answers, ask, "What if I showed them exactly how I think through problems?" or "What if I asked questions that demonstrated my strategic thinking?" Use the What If approach during interviews by asking thoughtful questions such as, "What if someone in this role could solve your biggest challenge?" This preparation approach helps you stand out by showing your thought process, not just your qualifications.

Build your professional reputation.

When looking to enhance how others see you, ask, "What if I became known as the person who helps others succeed?" or "What if I shared my knowledge more openly with teammates?" These questions help you develop a reputation as a valuable employee, collaborative team player, and natural mentor—qualities that accelerate career growth.

Explore entrepreneurial possibilities.

When considering starting your own business, ask, "What if I could solve a problem I deal with every day?" or "What if I leave my job in nine months to start my business?" These questions help you identify entrepreneurial opportunities that leverage your existing strengths and knowledge while creating realistic timelines for making the transition.

The What If career navigator sees possibility where others see only obstacles and uncertainty.

THE WHAT IF RULE IN ACTION: HEALTH AND WELLNESS

Health and wellness decisions often get stuck between good intentions and daily reality. Whether you're trying to build better habits, manage stress, or make lasting lifestyle changes, What If questions can transform your approach from all-or-nothing thinking to sustainable progress. Instead of waiting for motivation or the perfect plan, you can use What If thinking to create small shifts that compound into significant improvements over time.

Reframe your relationship with exercise.

When you dread working out or feel like you don't have time, ask, "What if I moved my body for just ten minutes today?" or "What if I found a type of exercise I actually enjoyed?" These questions help you discover sustainable ways to stay active without the pressure of perfect workout routines.

Make better food choices without perfectionism.

Instead of strict diets that lead to guilt, try asking, "What if I added one healthy thing to this meal?" or "What if, instead of grabbing that pizza to go, I found something healthy that I can eat in the car?" These questions create awareness around eating habits while avoiding the cycle of shame that derails most nutrition efforts.

Transform stress into strategic thinking.
When feeling overwhelmed, ask, "What if this stress is telling me something important?" or "What if I could take one action right now to reduce my stress?" These questions help you use stress as a source of information rather than letting it control your decisions and energy.

Build sustainable sleep habits.
When struggling with rest, try asking, "What if I created a thirty-minute wind-down routine?" or "What if better sleep was the key to solving my other challenges?" These questions help you prioritize rest as a foundation for everything else rather than something to sacrifice.

Create accountability without judgment.
When you slip up or struggle with consistency, ask, "What if I treated myself like I'd treat a good friend?" or "What if getting back on track was more important than being perfect?" These questions foster resilience and self-compassion, which support long-term change.

The What If approach to health fosters sustainable wellness rather than temporary fixes.

THE WHAT IF RULE IN ACTION: MONEY AND FINANCIAL DECISIONS

Money decisions often trigger fear, avoidance, or impulsive choices that don't align with your bigger goals. Whether you're managing daily expenses, planning for the future, or facing financial challenges, What If questions can transform your relationship with money from reactive to strategic. Instead of making financial choices based on scarcity or short-term thinking, you can use What If thinking to create clarity and confidence around your financial life.

Shift from scarcity to possibility thinking.

When money feels tight, ask, "What if I focused on creating value instead of just cutting costs?" or "What if there's an income opportunity I haven't considered?" These questions help you move beyond survival mode to see financial growth possibilities you might have missed.

Make intentional spending decisions.

Before making major purchases, try asking yourself, "What if I went without this?" or "What if I bought this with cash instead of credit?" These questions create space between impulse and action, helping you align your spending with your priorities and values.

Plan for the future without overwhelm.
When retirement or long-term goals feel impossible, ask, "What if I started with just 1 percent of my income?" or "What if I did something once a week to improve my financial future?" These questions make big financial goals feel achievable by breaking them into manageable steps.

Navigate financial setbacks strategically.
During financial struggles, try asking yourself, "What if I started doing something different with my money?" or "What if I could use this situation to build better financial habits?" These questions help you extract growth from difficult financial experiences rather than keep you stuck in shame or panic.

Start saving and investing consistently.
When building wealth feels overwhelming, ask, "What if I automated my savings so I never had to think about it?" or "What if I invested in my future self, starting with just $25 a week?" These questions help you begin building financial security through small, manageable actions that grow over time.

The What If approach to money fosters financial confidence rather than constant worry.

ABOUT DOUG FLEENER

Doug is a coach, speaker, and trusted adviser who helps individuals and companies apply the What If Rule to spark meaningful change and growth. His insights come from real transformation—going from a broke, out-of-work drug addict to director of retail for Bose Corporation, CEO of a national company, and a recognized expert on simple change and growth.

With over thirty years of experience in personal and professional growth, Doug's message is simple and powerful: You can always create better perspectives and options.

Through his speaking, coaching, and writing, Doug shows people how to harness the power of What If thinking to move forward, unlock possibilities, and achieve better outcomes in life and work.

To work with Doug:
Call or text: (617) 340-9041
Email: doug@dougfleener.com
Visit: www.DougFleener.com

FREE JOURNALING COURSE

There's a practice I use almost every day that has shaped who I am and how I live. I didn't include it in this book because I wanted Start With What If to stay focused on the What If Rule and the weekly questions.

But this other practice—Future Journaling—is equally important to me. Unlike traditional journaling, which often records what already happened, Future Journaling focuses on who you want to be and how you want to impact the people and world around you. It only takes a few minutes, but it's been life-changing for me.

That is why I created a free 3-day email course called Future Journaling. Each day, you'll get a short explanation and a simple journaling prompt. By the end of the three days, you'll have a tool you can carry forward for the rest of your life.

Sign up free at FutureJournaling.com.